회화를 위한 거꾸로 영문법

문법으로 회화를 확! 잡아주는 영어 강의

회화를 위한
거꾸로 영문법

이정아 지음

어문학사

Introduction

"영어를 10년이나 넘게 배우고도 제대로 말 한마디 못하는 게 말이 되나?" "TOEIC이 700~800 점대인데 회화는 영 안 돼!" "독해는 자신 있는데 말은 글쎄……?" 모순처럼 들리지만 그게 우리들의 현실이다. 요즘은 영어를 하도 강조하다 보니 제법 영어를 잘하는 젊은이들도 많지만 아직도 대다수의 한국인들은 영어 회화라면 두려움의 대상이다. 그리고 따로 돈 주고 회화 학원에 가서 배워야 하는 줄 안다. 왜 그럴까? 시중에 나와 있는 대부분의 영어 회화 교재들은 어떤 상황에서는 어떤 표현을 써야 하는지 친절히 예문을 제시하고 있다. 물론 알아두면 좋은 표현들이 많다. 그러나 실제 상황에서는 A가 이렇게 말하면 B가 꼭 그런 식으로 반응하지 않는다. 다시 말하면 얼마나 구어적인 표현을 많이 아느냐가 중요한 게 아니라 그때그때 상황에 맞게 자신의 생각을 표현할 수 있느냐가 중요하다. 물론 원어민처럼 자연스러운 표현을 쓰지는 못하더라도 기본적인 의사소통을 할 수 있을 정도로 표현할 줄 알면 구어적인 표현이나 자연스러운 표현은 2차적으로 배워나갈 수 있다.

본 교재는 우선 기본적인 영어 문법을 회화에 응용하기 위한 책이다. 그럼 왜 문법이 중요한가? 혹자들은 '회화와 문법은 별개야. 회화는 무조건 단어만 많이 알면 돼. 문법은 무시하고 그냥 떠들면 돼, 상황에 맞는 표현들을 무조건 외우면 돼'라고 말한다. 틀린 말은 아니다. 그러나 말은 생각을 표현하는 수단이고 상대에 따라 분위기에 따라 할 말이 달라진다. 영어 인터뷰를 준비해 본 사람은 상대가 자신이 준비한 대로만 질문하지 않으며, 준비된 표현이라도 질문의 의도에 따라 답변자가 방향을 바꾸어 대답해야 했던 걸 기억할 것이다. 회화는 외워서만은 할 수가 없다.

그럼 어떻게 하면 생각한 대로 말이 나올 수 있는가? 회화는 원어민들이 쓰는 표현 몇 가지만 외워서 되는 건 아니다. 영어를 외국어로 배우는 사람들에게 회화는 입으로 하는 작문이다. 다시 말해 문장을 상황에 맞게 계속해서 자연스럽게 생성해 내는 것이다. 어릴 때라면 굳이 문법을 배우지 않아도 문장구조가 익혀져서 문법에 맞는 문장이 자연스레 나오지만, 성인이 된 후에는 모국어와 많이 다른 문장구조를 배워야만 영어식 표현이 가능하다. 흔히 콩글리쉬라고 불리는 broken 영어는 영어식 문장구조에 익숙하지 않아 한국어 표현에 집착해서 생긴 부산물이다. 다시 한 번 강조하지만 영어식 문장구조를 익히는 것이 회화의 필수 요건이다. 영어식 문장구조는 문법에 기반한다.

한국어를 외국어로 배우는 외국인을 생각해보라. 그 외국인이 한국말 유행어 몇 마디 잘한다고 한국어가 유창하다고 말할 수 있는가? 단어만 많이 나열하면 잘한다고 할 수 있는가? 떠들긴 많이 하는데 우리말 문법이 엉망이라 무슨 말인지 이해가 불가능하다면 잘한다고 할 수 있는가? 한국인처럼 자연스러운 표현은 안 되더라도 또박또박 문법에 맞게 자기 생각을 표현할 수 있어야 비로소 의사소통이 된다. 영어를 외국어로 배우는 사람이라면, 영어를 할 때 한국어를 배우는 외국인을 반드시 생각하기 바란다. 이 책에서는 한국인이 영어로 생각을 표현하려면 어떻게 문법을 활용해야 하는지 재조명했다. 다시 말해 이 교재는 회화를 위한 영문법 활용 지침서인 셈이다.

본 교재에서는 Key structure를 통해 기본 문형을 제시하고, Extended expressions를 통해 기본 문형이 확장된 표현을 배운다. 가장 특징적인 것은 story telling 방식을 통해 기본 예문을 context로 기억할 수 있다는 것이다. Sample dialogue를 통해 기본 문형이 들어간 대화문을 공부하고, Pattern practice를 통해 기본 문형을 이용한 문장들을 반복해서 만들어 본다. Listening comprehension에서는 기본 pattern이 들어간 듣기 과제를 한 후, Reading comprehension에서는 기본 문형이 뉴스 등 실생활에서 어떻게 활용되는지 살펴본다. 뉴스에서 나온 주제를 가지고 토론을 진행하고 어떤 방향으로 이야기해야 할지 모르는 학생들을 위해 모범 답안을 실어 놓았다. 모범 답안을 통해 효과적으로 토론하는 법을 배울 수 있다. 이 책은 국내에서 영어 공부하는 학생은 물론 해외 어학 연수생에게도 큰 도움이 될 것으로 기대한다. 이 책을 통해 여러분의 영어 회화 능력이 성장하여 국제 사회에 걸맞은 경쟁력 있는 인재가 되기를 기원한다.

2013년 1월, 이정아

Table of Contents

- Introduction 4

	Topic	Grammar	Key Structure	
Unit 1	I have traveled Europe.	—Present Perfect	• Have + P.P. (Present Perfect)	8
Unit 2	She had her purse stolen.	—Causative Verbs/ Perceptive Verbs	• S + V (causative) + O (person) + O.C [R] • S + V + O (person) + O.C [to + R] • S + V + O (thing) + O.C [p.p.] • S + V (perceptive) + O (person) + O.C [R]	14
Unit 3	She is the girl who has wisdom.	—Relative Clause	• who + V, whose + N, who(m) + S + V • which + V, whose + N, which + S + V	22
Unit 4	If I were a superman, I could fly.	—Mood	• If + S + were, S + [would, should, could, might] + verb • If + S + had + p.p., S + [would, should, could, might] + have + p.p.	28
Unit 5	I have been learning how to cook Korean cuisine.	—Present Perfect Continuous	• Have + p.p. + —ing	34
Unit 6	She said that she would not go out.	—Reported Speech	• She said to me, "I will not go out." • He said to me, "do you like fish?" • He said to me, "who are you?"	40

Unit 7	I'm trying to eat less fat.	—Countable & Non-countable noun	• Uncountable Nouns • Countable Nouns	48
Unit 8	He is taller than his brother.	—Comparison	• Adjective + —er • More + adjective	54
Unit 9	What is the tallest mountain in the world?	—Superlative	• The + adjective + —est • The + most/least + adjective • Irregular Superlatives	62
Unit 10	He is a teacher, isn't he?	—Tag Question	• She is a teacher, isn't she? • He works for a bank, doesn't he? • It's been a while, hasn't it?	68
Unit 11	I enjoy dancing.	—Infinitive & Gerund	• S + V + —ing • S + V + to + R • S + V + to + R / —ing	74
Unit 12	A mouse is chased by a cat.	—Passive Voice	• S + V + O → S + be + p.p. + by + O	82
Unit 13	He must be his father.	—Auxiliary Verb	• cannot be ↔ must be • It + be + adjective + that + S + (should) + R = It + be + adjective + of + O + to + R • require, insist, order, suggest, desire, advise, decide + that + S + (should) + R	88
Unit 14	The man looking at the map is a tourist.	—Participle	• Modify noun before or after the noun • S + V + C / S + V + O + O.C	94

- Script & Answer Keys   101
- Acknowledgement   118

Unit 1: I have traveled Europe.

A KEY STRUCTURE

- Have + P.P. (Present Perfect)

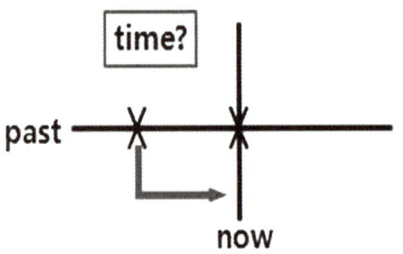
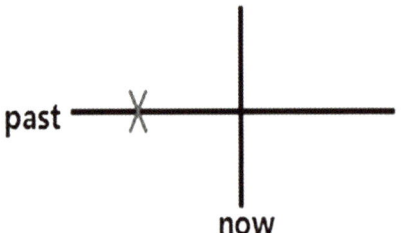

present perfect	simple past
unspecified time in the past	*specific time in the past*
• Things happened sometime in the past. —She has written books. (We don't know when exactly she wrote the books.) —I have traveled a lot. • Express experiences —Have you (ever) won a medal? —Has he gone to Europe? • The action is continued from sometime in the past until present. —They have learned English.	**Note**: p.p. cannot be used with the adverbial phrases indicating time. She wrote two books **in 2012**. I traveled a lot **this year**. Did you win a medal **last month**? **When** did he go to Jeju Island? They learned English **this summer**.

8 회화를 위한 거꾸로 영문법

B EXTENDED EXPRESSIONS

● Have + S + ever + p.p.

Have you ever kissed the girl?

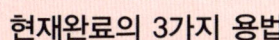

현재완료의 3가지 용법
① 불특정한 과거에 일어난 일을 표현할 때
　(시간을 나타내는 부사와 현재완료는 함께 쓰지 못함)
② 경험을 표현할 때
③ 과거의 동작이 현재까지 계속되어 올 때(현재완료의 계속 적용법)
　나중에 배울 현재완료진행과 비슷함: 현재완료진행에서는 진행의 의미가 강조

C SAMPLE DIALOGUE

A: Have you been to Europe?
B: Yes, I have. I have been to five countries in Europe.
A: Wow! Which countries have you been to?
B: I have been to France, Spain, Italy, Hungary and Britain.
A: *That sounds like fun.* [1]
B: Have you traveled by yourself?
A: Yes, I have. When I traveled to Jeju Island, I went there *all by myself.* [2]
B: Have you traveled abroad by yourself?
A: No, I haven't. I *was* a little bit *scared* to go overseas by myself. [3]
　But I will try *someday.* [4]

Note

[1] That sounds fun : 그거 재미있겠다
[2] all alone : 혼자
[3] become feared : 두려움을 느끼다
[4] sometime in the future : 언젠가

D PATTERN PRACTICE

(Let's play a board game!)

Directions

1. Form a group with four students.
2. Each group has a coin and each player has a marker. A small object can be used as a marker such as an eraser, a hair pin, a clip, etc.
3. Each player takes turns to flip a coin and moves the marker.
   (head → 1 space, tail → 2 spaces)
4. The player makes a sentence using the clue on the board.
5. The player who reaches the finish first wins the game.

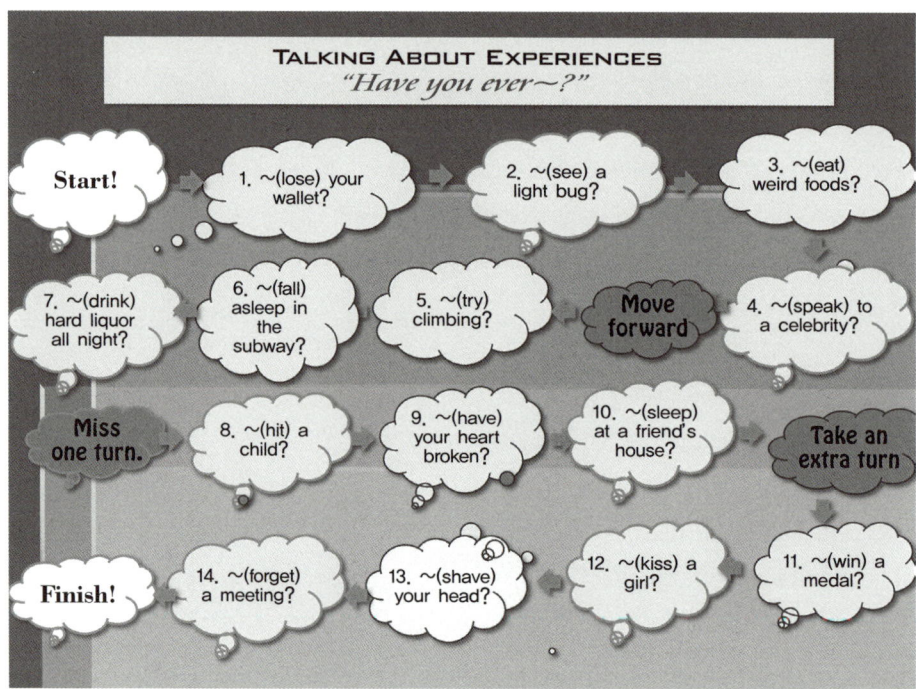

(Change the base form of verb into p.p.)

1. lose → lost
2. see → _____
3. eat → _____
4. speak → _____
5. try → _____
6. fall → _____
7. drink → _____
8. hit → _____
9. have → _____
10. sleep → _____
11. win → _____
12. kiss → _____
13. shave → _____
14. forget → _____

E LISTENING COMPREHENSION

1. What did she apologize to her boyfriend for?
2. What are the two things her friend suggests she do?
3. What is her friend's final advice?

F READING COMPREHENSION

(I have been to Mexico.)

I've been to Mexico quite a few times. My Grandmother used to live in Mexico and we would visit her almost every Mother's Day and Christmas. We had so much fun every time we visited my grandmother's house because it was always such a neat experience. Near my Grandmother's house, there was a beautiful old farm house where we could run around and play games. Now that I look back on those memories, it seems my imagination was never more active than when we played at that old farm house. We had so much fun chasing the chickens and the dogs all over the place. My sisters and I would pretend that we were farmers while we fed the animals and played in the fields.

Now that I think about, I have traveled quite a bit in my life. I have also been to Boston, New York and Washington D.C. on school field trips. Each of those trips was fun but none of them could compare with those trips that we took to our Grandmother's house in Mexico.

I have been to Las Vegas countless times. I lived about 2 hours away from Las Vegas when I was a college student so my friends and I would go there almost every weekend to catch a show or just to eat at the famous hotdog on the street. Sometimes we had too much fun in Las Vegas and it would be hard for us to calm back down and get back into our studies when Monday came around.

Comprehension Questions

1. What was the reason the author visited Mexico so many times?
2. What was the reason the author visited Boston, New York & Washington D.C.?
3. What was the reason the author visited Las Vegas?

Vocabulary List

school field trip : 수학여행
countless : 셀 수 없이 많은

Useful Expressions

used to~ : …하곤 했다

G SENTENCE BUILDING

1. 우리 교수님은 작년 겨울에 대학생을 위한 영어 문법책을 쓰셨습니다.
2. 저희 오빠는 지난 2월에 학원에서 상급자를 위한 컴퓨터 프로그램을 배웠습니다.

3. 저는 10년간 태권도를 배우고 있습니다.
4. 저는 지난 12년간 영어를 배워오고 있습니다.
5. 저는 영어권 국가에서 영어를 공부한 적이 있습니다.
6. 저는 프랑스에서 발레를 배웠어요.
7. 저는 공과대학에서 높은 수준의 컴퓨터 수업을 들은 적이 있습니다.
8. 저는 미국에 있을 때 바리스타 자격증을 취득했어요.
9. 저는 학교 수학여행으로 제주도에 가 보았습니다.
10. 저는 뉴욕에서 공부할 때 Washington D.C.를 방문한 적이 있습니다.

H DISCUSSION

(Stating about your experience)

The purpose of this discussion is to talk about your experience. Please use the key structure in Unit One when you debate.

(Issue)

What country or city have you visited? And why did you visit them?

(Opinion Sample)

I have visited Busan for a school field trip when I was a high school student. I stayed there for three nights and four days. *I have visited museums*, ports, and custom offices. It was so much fun and informative. If I have another chance to visit Busan, I would love to go there again.

Unit 2: She had her purse stolen.

A. KEY STRUCTURE

- S + V (causative) + O (person) + O.C [R]

> make, have, let, bid

Meaning: force/order someone to do something

Nothing makes me change my mind.
My parents make me come home before 10 O'clock.
The news made me cry.
Nancy had her boyfriend do her homework.
I will let you borrow my computer. (let→ permission)

- S + V + O (person) + O.C [to + R]

> get, want, ask, cause, tell, command, order, urge,
> want, persuade, enable, invite, require, expect

Meaning: manage to persuade

I got my husband to pick me up at the airport.
I got my professor to put the midterm off.
My daughter always wants me to pay the bill.
My mother often asks me to answer the phone.
My grandfather always tells me to speak louder.
I helped her (to) peel the apple.

*The verb 'Help' may take the basic form of verb instead of to-infinitives.

- S + V + O (thing) + O.C [p.p.]

  Meaning: When a thing comes as an object, the relationship between object and object complement is passive.

  He had his wallet stolen.
  She had her hair cut.
  I had the car repaired.
  He made the roof fixed.

  cf) The causative verb 'have'
  I had Michael fix the car.
  (I arranged for the car to be fixed by Michael—I caused him to fix it.)

  I had the car fixed.
  (I arranged for the car to be fixed by someone. We don't know who)

- S + V (perceptive) + O (person) + O.C [R]

  > see, hear, feel, behold, perceive, overhear

  Meaning: When the perceptive verb comes, object complement uses the base form of verb.

  I overhear him speak.
  I saw her come into the building.
  I heard him see someone. (*'see someone' means dating with someone)
  I heard my mom yell at my brother.

B EXTENDED EXPRESSIONS

- S + V (perceptive) + O + O.C [ing] 능동의 의미 (instrument or sports game)
  I saw her playing the violin.
- S + V (perceptive) + O + O.C [ed] 수동의 의미

I saw her scolded by her teacher.

사역동사의 4가지 용법
① 강제의 의미를 가진 경우: 목적보어가 원형
② 부탁의 의미를 가진 경우: 목적보어가 to 부정사
③ 목적어인 사물과 목적보어의 관계가 수동인 경우: 목적보어가 p.p.
④-⑴ 지각동사인 경우: 목적보어가 원형
　-⑵ 지각동사인데 연주, 경기 등이 목적보어로 올 때: 목적보어가 -ing
　-⑶ 지각동사인데 목적어와 목적보어의 관계가 수동인 경우: 목적보어가 p.p.

C SAMPLE DIALOGUE

A: *Why do you have such a long face?* [1]
B: I *had my wallet stolen*.
A: How did it happen?
B: I was in a crowded subway and watching TV dramas on my Smartphone.
A: So you didn't notice somebody stealing your wallet.
B: Yeah! I *should have paid* more *attention* in a *public place*. [2] [3] [4]
A: *It is what it is.* [5] You need to go to a *refreshing atmosphere*. [6] Let's go out for a drink.
B: *Are you sure you want to* drink *so soon after* your *hangover* last week? [7] [8]
A: Yeah! You are right! *I am not in a position to* give you advice. [9]

▶ **Note**

[1] Why are you so sad? : Why do you look so sad?
[2] should have p.p. : …했었어야 했는데 (과거에 못한 일에 대한 후회)
[3] pay attention : 주의를 기울이다
[4] public place : 공공장소
[5] 세상은 다 그런 거야, 원래 그런 거야
[6] 신선한 분위기, 기분 전환
[7] hangover : 숙취

[8] Are you sure you want to—so soon after—? : 그렇게 빨리 …하고 싶어?
[9] I am not in a position to— : 할 처지가 아니다

D PATTERN PRACTICE

Fill in the blank using the given words and complete the sentence.

1. He has his assistant _____ his papers. (type)
2. My father often helped my mom _____ the dishes. (wash)
3. I had my roommate _____ his room. (clean)
4. I got my dress _____. (alter)
5. I watch him _____ baseball. (play)
6. I saw him _____ by a robber. (rob)
7. I heard him _____ at his son. (yell)
8. She had her purse _____. (stole)
9. My parents made me _____ back home by 10 p.m. (come)
10. My grandma always tells me _____ louder. (speak)

E LISTENING COMPREHENSION

Listen to the conversation and complete the chart using the given information.

	Job	Exercise	Friend
Old			
Current			

F READING COMPREHENSION

A movie star battles back after addiction

Mr. Kim battled the demons of addiction and public embarrassment to recover joy in his profession and his personal life. Mr. Kim won the Dajonsang Film Award in 1998 and was nominated for the best leading actor at the Cannes Film Festival in 2001. But it has been a rough road, even for a person who learned to work hard as a little boy on the family farm. "I like seeing a beautiful finished product," said Mr. Kim, 48. "I still monitor my own acting and try to find a way to improve it. Every time I have a different role, I'm so excited," he said, clapping his hands. "It's my pleasure to *see my fans happy and get them to see my film. My fans made me change my life.* Life hasn't always been so much fun," he said.

Comprehension Questions

1. What is Mr. Kim's occupation?
2. What award did he win?
3. Why was he in a news report?

Vocabulary List

battle : fight between opposing armies, naval or air forces, etc. or people : 전쟁, 전투, 싸움
demons : an evil spirit : 악마, 악령
addiction : the state of being addicted : 열중, 탐닉, 중독
embarrassment : 당황함
clapping one's hands : 박수치다

G SENTENCE BUILDING

1. 난 남자친구에게 영어숙제를 대신하게 시켰다.
2. 난 다음 주 금요일까지 내 차를 고치게 시켰다.
3. 남편에게 딸을 유치원에 데려다 달라고 부탁했다.
4. 선생님에게 시험을 학기 말까지 연기하게 만들었다.
5. 우리 학교는 일주일에 한 번 채플에 참석하기를 의무사항으로 만들었어요.
6. 제 여자친구가 피아노 치는 것을 보았어요.
7. 전 아빠가 지붕 고치는 것을 도왔습니다.
8. 우리 가족은 그가 강도들에게 얻어맞는 것을 보았어요.
9. 저는 우리 누나가 저한테 소리 지르는 것을 들었지만 대답도 하지 않았습니다.
10. 전 혼잡한 버스 안에서 제 배낭을 도둑맞았어요.

H DISCUSSION

(Why or Why not?)

The purpose of this discussion is to demonstrate how to support or oppose an argument. Please use the key structure in Unit Two when you debate.

(Issue)

A lot of people believe that physical appearance is important in social life. Would you get cosmetic surgery? Why or why not?

(Opinion Sample)

i) I agree that physical appearance is important in social life. I would like to get cosmetic surgery if I have enough money. I believe that *cosmetic surgery could make me look better. Better physical appearance enables me to get a better job*.

ii) I don't think physical appearance is everything. Also, I guess *cosmetic surgery could make me look unnatural*. I prefer the natural beauty. *The knowledge in my profession enables me to be an expert* not my physical appearance. Therefore, I would not get cosmetic surgery in any circumstances.

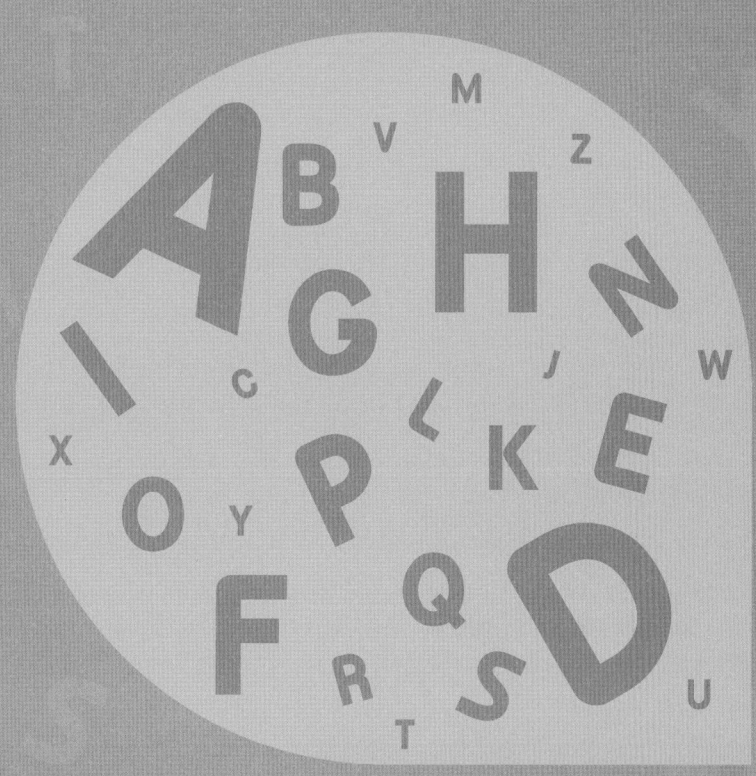

Unit 3 She is the girl who has wisdom.

A KEY STRUCTURE

	사람	사물
1. 주격	who + V	which + V
2. 소유격	whose + N	whose + N
3. 목적격	who(m) + S + V	which + S + V

1. *This is the girl who is a good student.*
2. *Look at the book whose cover is red.*
3. *This is the house which she lives in.*

B EXTENDED EXPRESSIONS

- A is to B what (as) C is to D = What C is to D, A is to B
  Meaning : A가 B에 대한 관계는 C가 D에 대한 관계와 같다.
  Reading is to the soul what as food is to the body.

- what one has (재산), what one is (인격)
  She loves me not for what I have, but for what I am.

- no – but = that – not (no)
  There is no rule but has exceptions.
  = *There is no rule that has no exceptions.*

C SAMPLE DIALOGUE

Background information
Close friends run into each other at an unexpected place. [1]

A: Hey! *You are the last person whom I expected to meet here.* [2] *What brought you here?* [3]
B: I just *stop by* to meet my girlfriend. [4]
A: You have a girlfriend? Why didn't you tell me?
B: I just didn't have a chance.
A: *What is she like?* [5]
B: She is the girl who has both wisdom and beauty at the same time. She is the girl whose personality just fits mine. Her name is Laura. Oh! *Speak of the devil.* [6]
(A girlfriend approaches the guys.)
A: You *must be* Laura. [7] Nice to meet you. *I've heard many good things about you.* [8]

Note
[1] happen to meet : 우연히 만나다
[2] 여기서 만나리라곤 생각 못했어.
[3] 여긴 어쩐 일이야?
[4] stop by, drop by, come by : 들르다
[5] ask about the personality : 어떤 사람이야? / 어떻게 생겼어? What does she look like?
[6] someone shows up when people are talking about him/her : 호랑이도 제 말 하면 오네
[7] must be : …임에 틀림없어
[8] 네 얘기 많이 들었어.

D PATTERN PRACTICE

> Combine each pair of sentences using "who, whose, that, or which". More than one answer may be possible.

1. I have a friend. She calls me a lot to talk about her boyfriend.
   _____.

2. I made some new friends at a hobby club. It organizes hiking trips.
   _____.

3. My best friend has a guitar. She bought it from a singer.
   _____.

4. I know someone. He throws a big party once a year.
   _____.

5. I have a really interesting friend. I met him at my college.
   _____.

6. I found the cool Web site. It helps you to find your old friends.
   _____.

7. Carolina is someone. I can trust her.
   _____.

8. Nina is a woman. Her son is a rebel.
   _____.

9. Jenny talks about the things. She is doing the things.
   _____.

10. She had a company. The company planned weddings.
    _____.

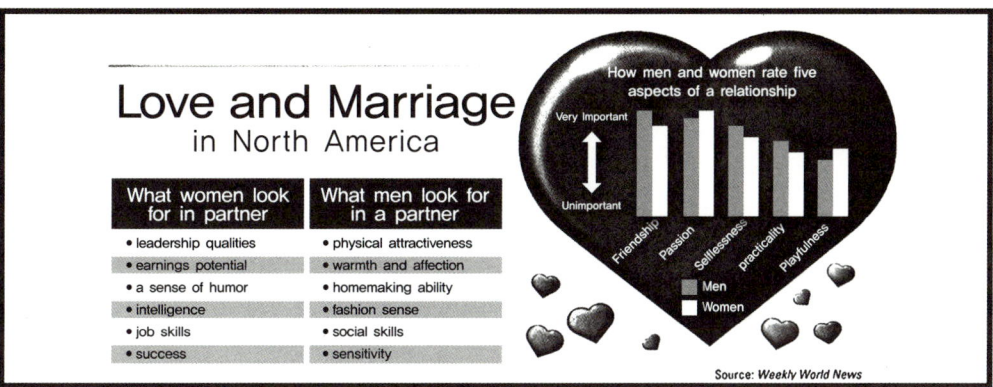

Which of the qualities above is the most important for you to look for in a partner? Are there other important qualities missing from the lists?

Sample Dialogue

A: What is the most important quality when you look for guys?

B: For me, the most important quality is physical attractiveness. I like guys who are clean-cut. How about you?

A: Well, I'd prefer someone who is intelligent. I like smart people.

E LISTENING COMPREHENSION

Listen to Alex talk about the three people below. What contrasting information does he give about each person? Complete the sentences.

1. The clerk at a café gets stressed out. She's very _____, though.
2. My computer teacher is really nice. He's kind of _____, though.
3. My yoga instructor is incredibly easy going. She can be a bit _____, though.

F READING COMPREHENSION

(A seven-year-old *girl who died* at the church in front of her family)

A seven-year-old girl was killed in Sacramento, California when a large cross fell off and hit her head. Police have not yet identified the specific reason for the death, but they say she was trying to move the cross in church. The girl was at the church with two other siblings and their *mother who was not present* when the terrible accident happened, according to the local news. The little girl's siblings were at the horrific scene when it took place around 2 p.m. Wednesday. Another parishioner *who knows* the family told the news reporter, "I'm very upsetting why it happens to an innocent girl."

(Comprehension Questions)

1. What is speculated for the reason of the death?
2. Who was at the accident scene?

(Vocabulary List)

identify : to recognize someone or something as being a particular person or thing; to establish their or its identity : 감식하다, 인정하다
parish : a district or area served by its own church and priest or minister, usually the established church of that particular area : 소교구, 지역 교구
siblings : a blood relation; a brother or sister : 형제자매
parishioner : a member or inhabitant of a parish : 소교구민

G SENTENCE BUILDING

1. 저에게는 밤늦게 전화하는 친구가 있습니다.
2. 해외여행을 조직하는 모임에서 몇 사람을 만났습니다.

3. 제 친구는 저자로부터 직접 서명을 받은 책이 있습니다.
4. 자신의 여자친구에게 큰 생일파티를 열어준 남자를 알고 있습니다.
5. 전 영어수업에서 만난 굉장히 재미있는 친구가 있습니다.
6. 전 일자리를 찾는 것을 도와주는 기업체를 찾았어요.
7. 제 어머니는 어떤 상황에서도 제가 신뢰할 수 있는 분입니다.
8. 저는 망나니 남동생이 있는 여자를 알아요.
9. 제 친구는 만날 때마다 현재 자신이 하고 있는 아르바이트 얘기를 해요.
10. 그녀는 직원들의 교육을 지원해주는 회사에 다녀요.

H DISCUSSION

Persuasion

Making a persuasive case is the purpose of this discussion. Please use the key structure in Unit Three when you debate.

Issue

Your child needs constant care and supervision. Your husband thinks a seven-year-old girl is mature enough to take care of herself. Persuade him to realize that a seven-year-old girl is young and needs constant care and supervision.

Opinion Sample

Just look at the news article. *Young children who are exposed to danger* without parents' supervision easily get into accidents. They seem to be independent; but they are not yet responsible for their own actions. Sometimes young children act first before they think. Parents are responsible to be with their young children under all circumstances and protect them from all possible danger. A seven-year-old boy or girl is not mature enough to judge the situation properly.

Unit 4 If I were a superman, I could fly.

A KEY STRUCTURE

- If + S + were ~, S + [would, should, could, might] + verb
  Meaning : to talk about impossible or unlikely situation
  If I were a superman, I could fly.

- If + S + had + p.p., S + [would, should, could, might] + have + p.p.
  Meaning : to express regret that you couldn't do in the past
  If he had arrived earlier, he could have met her.

B EXTENDED EXPRESSIONS

- If + S + had p.p., S + [would, could, might] + R
  Meaning : condition in the past, the result in present.
  If I had studied English hard, I would be fluent in English now.

- I wish + S + were
  I wish I were a bird.

- I wish + S + had + p.p.
  I wish I had gone to the beach.

- as if + S + past tense
  He ignores me as if I were invisible.

- **as if + S + had + p.p.**

  I felt so comfortable to be with him as if we had met before.

C SAMPLE DIALOGUE

A: *You look so upset.* [1] What happened?

B: My boyfriend just *stood* me *up*. [2]

A: Wait a minute. *I happened to meet John* at the subway station five minutes ago. [3] He said he had to go back home because he forgot to turn off the gas.

B: Oh, No! If I had arrived five minutes earlier, I might have met him.

A: It's not your fault.

B: Yes it is. *Actually*, I was 30 minutes late. [4]

A: If I were you, I would call him right away.

Note

[1] What made you so upset?

[2] I am being stood up : 바람맞다

   He was making me wait for him; but he didn't show up.

[3] I accidently met John.

[4] As a matter of fact, In fact : 사실은

D PATTERN PRACTICE

Find the appropriate words from the box and change the form to complete the sentence. (There are some extra words.)

come, apply, meet, get, study, have,
ask, make, be, answer, take

Example

If I had had experiences in that field, I would have applied for the job.

1. If I had arrived at the subway station earlier, I could have _____ my friend.
2. He would have gotten along well with his colleagues if he had _____ nice.
3. I would have _____ more work done if I had not taken too many breaks.
4. If he had _____ more money, she would have been happier.
5. If I had not liked the TV program, I would have _____ my roommate to change the channel.
6. If I had been in a class, I would not have _____ the phone.
7. If he had _____ on time, I might have talked to him.
8. If I had studied English when I was a high school student, I would _____ fluent in English now.
9. If I had arrived earlier, he would _____ married her.
10. If I had _____, I could have passed the exam.

E LISTENING COMPREHENSION

Listen to the paragraph and complete the chart using the given information.

	Cost of transportation	Cost of lodging	Total cost
By plane			
By plain a week ahead			
By train			

F READING COMPREHENSION

We'll never know what *might have happened*

I've been the owner of a convenience store in Indiana for 15 years. I've had one friend killed and another storeowner I knew was severely pistol-whipped by armed robbers. It is quite common to have armed robbers at a convenience store. We don't really know what the robber in the news *would have done* if shots had not been fired by the young store clerk. The store clerk was interviewed immediately after the robbery while his adrenaline was pumped. He said that he did what he had to do at that moment. If he had not shot the robber, would the robber have killed someone in the store? We'll never know. But to convict a person of murder for shooting armed robber is not right. Even though the armed robber did not shoot anyone in the store, someone *would have been* killed, if the young store clerk did not fire. I'm ashamed of the court's decision.

Comprehension Questions

1. What happened in a convenience store in the news?
2. Why is the author angry about the court?

Vocabulary List

pistol-whip : to hit someone with a pistol : 권총으로 맞은

armed : supplied with arms (weapons) : 무장한
conviction : the act of convicting; an instance of being convicted : 유죄판결
while his adrenaline was pumped : 아직 그가 몹시 흥분되어 있을 때
adrenaline-charged : (영화·게임·활동 따위가) 자극적인, 손에 땀을 쥐게 하는

G SENTENCE BUILDING

1. 만약 내가 아르바이트 경험이 있었더라면 그 회사의 인턴으로 뽑혔을 텐데.
2. 학교에 일찍 도착했었더라면 영어 수업을 들을 수 있었을 텐데.
3. 그가 우호적이었다면 친구들과 잘 어울려 지낼 수 있었을 텐데.
4. 스터디 그룹에 가입했었더라면 지금쯤 해외에 갈 수 있었을 텐데.
5. 커피를 너무 많이 마시지 않았더라면 지금 바로 잠들 수 있을 텐데.
6. 히말라야 산에 갔었으면 좋았을 텐데.
7. 그는 내가 마치 가정부인 것처럼 취급한다.
8. 난 마치 우리가 전에 얘기를 나눴었던 것처럼 그녀와 있는 게 아주 편하게 느껴졌다.
9. 내가 만약 너의 경우라면 난 지갑을 경찰서에 가져다줄 텐데.
10. 내가 슈퍼맨이라면 좋을 텐데.

H DISCUSSION

Pros and Cons

The purpose of this discussion is effectively to defend or refute an opinion. Please use the key structure in Unit Four when you debate.

Issue

If the armed robbers came into my store, I would shoot the armed robbers even if they didn't attack me.

i) How would you support this issue?
ii) How would you criticize this issue?

> **Opinion Sample**

i) I think I *would have shot* the armed robbers before they attack me. When the armed robbers break into my store, they already had an intention to harm people to achieve their goal, which getting money. I have to think about *what might have happened*, if I *had not taken* an action. Therefore, it is justified to shoot the armed robbers.

ii) I think it is not right to shoot the people just because they are armed. They *might have left* without any trouble, if you *had not attacked* them. Violence leads to more violence. Therefore, I think you should not shoot people if they don't attack you first.

Unit 5: I have been learning how to cook Korean cuisine.

A KEY STRUCTURE

- Have + p.p. + −ing

    Meaning: keep doing things from a certain point in the past

    I have been learning English for 11 years.

B EXTENDED EXPRESSIONS

- How long + have + S + been + −ing

    How long have you been living here/there?
    How long have you been working in L.A.?

C SAMPLE DIALOGUE

A: Hello, Peter. *What can I do for you?*[1]

B: *I was wondering if I could ask* for *a* small *favor.*[2][3]

A: All right. What is it?

B: Well, I have been working at a restaurant as my part-time job most evenings.

A: Yes.

B: Um, I haven't finished my term paper yet, and it's due on Friday.

A: Uh—huh.

B: So, I want to ask if I could have a few more days to finish it.

34 회화를 위한 거꾸로 영문법

A: Well, I really can't do that, Peter. If I give you more time, it isn't fair to your classmates. You know what I mean?

B: Yes, I understand. I'll *take off* work tonight so I can finish the paper. [4]

Note

[1] How can I help you?
[2] I was wondering if— : …해도 됩니까?
[3] ask a favor : 호의를 베풀다
[4] take off : 빼다

D PATTERN PRACTICE

(Let's play a board game!)

Directions

1. Form a group with four students.
2. Each group has a coin and each player has a marker. A small object can be used as a marker such as an eraser, a hair pin, a clip, etc.
3. Each player takes turns to flip a coin and moves the marker.
   (head → 1 space, tail → 2 spaces)
4. The player makes a sentence using the clue on the board.
5. The player who reaches the finish first wins the game.

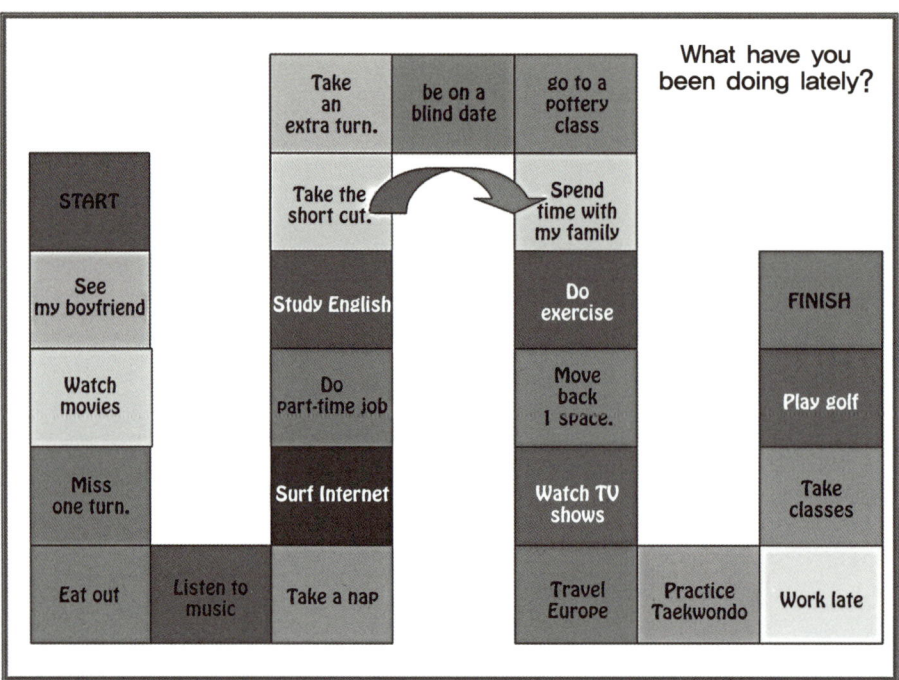

E   LISTENING COMPREHENSION

> Listen to Timothy read a review of Ringling Bros. Circus. Check whether the sentences are true or false. Correct the false sentences.

1. Ringling Bros. Circus performers are all Canadian.   T   F
2. The group started over 100 years ago.   T   F
3. They now perform all over the world.   T   F
4. The acrobats do not perform with animals.   T   F
5. Timothy has already seen a Ringling Bros. Circus show.   T   F
6. Timothy is going to call to find out about tickets.   T   F

F READING COMPREHENSION

I have been learning Korean cuisine bridging generations and cultures

Food says so much about where you've come from and the lessons you've learned. It's geography, politics, tradition, belief and so much more. Sitting over a steaming bowl of bibimbap, Catherin Kim recalled her father's cardinal rule when it came to food. He didn't feel like he'd had a good meal if it isn't served while it is hot. Kim said she used to hold a chunk of rice between chopsticks over her steaming bowl and waited for it to cool. Piping hot dishes with an extra spicy are staples of Korean cuisine that characterize the first-generation Korean Americans. Maybe, her heart is linked to the traditions of her family; but her palate has been tempered by nearly a lifetime in the United States. "*I have been learning* how to cook Korean cuisine lately because it reminds me of my childhood and bridges my parents' generation and me. I love Korean food as I grow older and I feel just as much at home with Korean food," said Kim, whose family moved to the United States when she was three.

Vocabulary List

geography : the scientific study of the Earth's surface, especially its physical features, climate, resources, population, etc. : 지리학
cardinal : any of the most important : 가장 중요한
chunk : a thick, especially irregularly shaped, piece : 덩어리
staple : principal; main : 주성분
palate : the roof of the mouth : 입천장, 미각
tempered : 조절된, 길들여진
remind A of B : A에게 B를 상기시키다

Comprehension Questions

1. According to the author, what are two characteristics of Korean food?
2. Why has she been learning Korean cuisine?

G SENTENCE BUILDING

1. 그는 같은 고등학교를 졸업한 여자와 데이트 중이야.
2. 지난 10년 동안 태권도를 배워왔어.
3. 미국에서 얼마나 오랫동안 살아왔니?
4. 얼마나 오랫동안 요가를 해왔니?
5. 영어수업을 얼마나 오랫동안 들어왔니?
6. 얼마나 자주 영어 회화수업을 들어왔니?
7. 영어수업시간에 비디오를 봐오고 있어.
8. 난 요즘 늦게까지 일하고 있어.
9. 난 이틀에 한 번 운동을 하고 있어.
10. 난 편의점에서 점원으로 아르바이트를 하고 있어.

H DISCUSSION

(Do you know how?)

Contriving solutions to a serious issue is the purpose of this discussion. Please use the key structure in Unit Five when you debate.

(Issue)

A great number of second-generation Korean-Americans do not know the Korean language and culture. This phenomenon has disastrous effects on bridging the gap between the first generation and their descendants. How can we fix the problem?

(Opinion Sample)

We need to do two things. First, provide practical incentives for the person who understands both languages. One of the major reasons of avoiding learning their heritage language is money. The Korean government should be financially responsible and provide monetary incentives to the second generation Korean Americans for learning the Korean language. Second, offer more jobs for Korean-Americans in either the U.S. or Korea. Those who want to work using both languages should be able to find a job easily. Then, people will want to learn the Korean language more and the social problems will be resolved.

Unit 6 She said that she would not go out.

A KEY STRUCTURE

● She said to me, "I will not go out."
  She told me that she would not go out.

평서문일 때 직접 화법의 주어가 간접 화법일 경우 문장 시작 주어와 일치하게 바뀌고 직접 화법의 동사가 간접 화법일 경우 문장 시작 동사의 시제와 일치한다.

● He said to me, "do you like fish?"
  He asked me if I like fish.

의문문일 때 일반동사의 경우 직접 화법에서는 do로 시작하나 간접 화법의 경우 접속사가 if로 바뀜.

● He said to me, "who are you?"
  He asked me who I was.

의문문일 때 직접 화법에서는 의문사로 시작하면 간접 화법의 경우 접속사는 의문사 그대로 씀.

B EXTENDED EXPRESSIONS

● She said to me, "could you give me some sugar?"
  She asked me to give her some sugar.

공손한 표현을 위한 조동사(could, would) 사용일 경우 조동사, 주어를 생략하고 to-부정사로 연결한다.

- She said, "God bless my son!"
  She prayed that God might bless her son.
  감탄문, 기도문 등의 경우 의미상 필요한 동사를 써준다.

- He said to me, "come to the principal's office."
  He told me that I come to his office.
  명령문의 경우 생략된 주어를 찾아 문맥상 의미에 맞게 쓴다.

- He said, "let's celebrate the victory tonight."
  He proposed to celebrate the victory that night.
  의미상 필요한 동사를 써준다.
  시간을 나타내는 부사도 간접 의문문으로 바뀔 때 시제 변화를 따라 한다.
  tonight → that night
  now → then

- [감탄문] He said, "What a brave boy he is!"
  He exclaimed that he was a very brave boy.
  He said, "What a 형용사 + 명사 + 대명사 + 동사"
  → He exclaimed that 대명사 + 동사 + a + very + 형용사 +명사

C SAMPLE DIALOGUE

A: Hi! Julia. Why are you so *dressed up*?[1]
B: Oh, I just came from an interview. It was with an airline company.
A: So *how did it go*?[2]

B: It was awful, and I was nervous.

A: That's natural. So, tell me, what kind of questions did they start with?

B: Oh, they asked me what part-time jobs I've had, and what I was studying at college. And they asked me what my strongest and weakest points were.

A: So let me guess. You told them you didn't have any weak points, right?

B: No, I was honest and told them my weak point is that I am shy. Also, one of the interviewers asked me what kind of people I *get along with*.[3]

B: I said I got along well with people who have a good sense of humor. But it seems that they didn't like my answer. They didn't smile.

A: Well, sounds like that's not the answer they wanted to hear; but I believe that you are definitely a *reliable* person.[4]

B: Thank you. Wish me good luck! *I'll just cross my fingers*.[5]

Note

[1] dress up : 차려입다
[2] What was it like? : 어땠니?
[3] get along well with : (누구와) 잘 어울리다
[4] dependable : 믿을만한
[5] I'll just cross my fingers : 행운을 빌어줘

D PATTERN PRACTICE

(I. Convert the direct speech into reported speech.)

1. He said to her, "you may go."
   →

2. She said to me, "could you call me later?"
   →

3. He said, "who did you talk to?"
   →

4. He said to me, "come to my office now."
   →

5. He said, "let's celebrate my promotion tonight."
   →

6. She said, "What a beautiful sight it is!"
   →

7. The man said, "Oh! It was all my fault."
   →

8. The student said, "Hurrah! I passed the exam."
   →

9. She said, "I wish I passed the exam."
   →

10. She said, "I will not go out tonight, because it is raining."
    →

II. Complete the conversation based on what Lisa answers.

Michelle: I think I've found the man of my dream.
Lisa: What! How do you know?
Michelle: Well, I asked him if _____ (1).
Lisa: And he said he loved extreme sports!
Michelle: Yes, he did. Then I asked him if _____ (2).
Lisa: Don't tell me he said he loved animals, especially reptiles!
Michelle: Yes, he did. The best was when I asked him if _____ (3).
Lisa: Don't tell me he said he wasn't seeing anybody!
Michelle: He didn't say that, but there's no harm in dreaming.
Lisa: Oh, please!

III. Make reported questions.

Harry   Alicia   Tony&Lisa   Hector

1. "I'm looking forward to the election."
   Harry said _____
2. "I don't care about elections and presidents."
   Alicia _____
3. "We want to talk to Alicia about the importance of voting."
   Tony and Lisa _____
4. "I won't vote because I can't vote online."
   Hector said that _____

E LISTENING COMPREHENSION

Christina is telling her father about her day. Listen to the conversation and check the sentences T (true) or F (false).

1. Christina had a chance to talk to one of the IT experts at a career fair.   T   F
2. The company hires only experienced employees each year.   T   F
3. Christina had a clear plan for what she wants to do after graduation.   T   F
4. Christina wants to work overseas.   T   F
5. Jason called her but he didn't leave a message.   T   F

F READING COMPREHENSION

> She is putting her life on hold after her fiancé's murder.

Ethan and I were a high school sweetheart. We fell in love and planned to get married when I was junior at college. But the Lord gave me new dreams. It was before I turned 22 when it happened. Ethan was an Intern for his summer job, and he left the office to get everybody soft drinks. A guy who had been fired from his job shot Ethan. He had only a cursory knowledge of who Ethan was.

I think divine intervention changed my life and set me on a different course. After Ethan was killed, I had to learn how to control my thoughts. I was suffered from extreme depression. After five years when the incident happened, I wished I had been strong enough to relive the whole thing and let go the past. Even years later, I really had a hard time entertaining the thought of allowing myself to have a family.

What happened is one night I had a dream. I had a dream about Ethan. I met him in a subway station. He was waiting for me, and I sat down next to him. In the dream, *he said he was in heaven, and he wanted me to go on*. I got up and looked back at him, and he gestured for me to go. That next morning *I called my boyfriend, David, and said," You've got to move to New York! It's time for us to go for broke."* We got married and I had twins now.

I will always believe that somewhere in this universe Ethan still exists. I don't believe love goes away just because you're buried in the ground. And one thing I've learned is it is important to pass on to crime victims a message that there is still happiness in the world. And it will come to you. You just have to let it in.

> Comprehension Questions

Read the paragraph and check the sentences T (true) or F (false).
1. Keith was murdered by a man who was fired from his school.   T   F
2. Keith and the murderer were close friends.   T   F
3. Keith felt guilty to get married to another man.   T   F
4. The dream about her ex-boyfriend made her move on.   T   F
5. Keith learned that crime victims can be happy again.   T   F

Vocabulary List

put on hold : 대기상태에 두다
cursory : a brief one in which you do not pay much attention to detail : 대충하는, 피상적인
divine : discover or learn it by guessing : 알다, 예측하다
intervention : the act of intervening in a situation : 개입

G SENTENCE BUILDING

1. 제 상사는 제게 가도 좋다고 말했습니다.
2. 제 남자친구는 제게 나중에 전화하라고 부탁했어요.
3. 제 여자친구는 제가 전화하는 것을 듣고 누구와 통화했냐고 물었어요.
4. 교수님께서 저에게 그때 연구실에 들르라고 말씀하셨어요.
5. 운동선수는 그날 밤 승리를 축하하자고 제안했다.
6. 2년 전 그랜드캐니언을 방문했을 때, 난 너무나 아름다운 경치라며 함성을 질렀다.
7. 제 친구는 최근에 남자친구와 헤어졌는데 한숨 섞인 목소리로 모든 게 자기 잘못이라고 했습니다.
8. 그 학생은 기쁨에 넘치며 아나운서가 되기 위한 인터뷰에 합격했다고 말했습니다.
9. 전 제 여동생이 수능시험(college entrance exam)에 합격했으면 좋겠다고 소원했습니다.
10. 저는 지난 토요일 밤에 비가 오기 때문에 나가지 않겠노라고 말했습니다.

H DISCUSSION

Is this true?

The purpose of this discussion is to examine common beliefs that many people have strong opinions about. Judging whether or not the common beliefs are actually true is the key for the discussion. Please use the key structure in Unit Six when you debate.

Issue

I have heard it said that crime victims suffered from severe mental traumas. Do you think this is true?

Opinion Sample

I believe the statement is true. Reflecting on my own experience of losing my friend at an accident, I felt guilty about the fact that I did not stop him. I guess most of people have the same feeling when a horrible incident happened. Even though the crime victim knows it was not his or her fault, it seems like he or she feels responsible for what happened. In general, *the crime victims said that they would not go out and meet people for a while.* Cases where one loses a close friend generally lead to negative thoughts. Unfortunately, crime victims are emotionally affected and this can be said to be the secondary effects of crime. Therefore, it is very important to offer counseling services for crime victims after the incident.

Unit 7: I'm trying to eat less fat.

A KEY STRUCTURE

- **Uncountable Nouns**

  Korean food has very little fat.
  There's very little food.
  I'm trying to eat less red meat.
  There's not much food in the fridge.

- **Countable Nouns**

  We have a few slices of cheese.
  We eat very few frozen meals.
  Low fat milk has fewer calories.
  There aren't many vegetables.

  fruit / vegetable
  과일, 야채(전체를 총칭할 때나 식품으로서의 과일 야채는 단수 집합명사, 종류를 나타낼 때는 보통명사 취급)

B EXTENDED EXPRESSIONS

- **Food containers**

  A carton of milk → two cartons of milk
  A bag of rice → two bags of rice

C SAMPLE DIALOGUE

A: Cathy, *is this your third dish?*[1]
B: Yeah, it is. I really love this stuff. It's my favorite dessert.
A: If I were you, I wouldn't eat so much. It has too much fat and not enough *fiber*.[2]
B: I know. You're right. It's not healthy. But it's so good.
A: Everybody's trying to eat less fat. What happened to you?
B: I just love the taste besides there is not much food in my *refrigerator*.[3]
A: Come on. If you want to be healthy, there is healthy food everywhere.
B: I have only a few slices of bread in my fridge. There's nothing like better than this butter-finger.
A: Oh, *you are helpless*![4]

Note
[1] 세 번째 먹는 거니?
[2] 식이섬유
[3] 냉장고
[4] 넌 어쩔 수 없구나!

D PATTERN PRACTICE

I. Complete the sentences with too, too much, too many, or enough.

1. I eat _____ fast food and not _____ fruit and vegetables.
2. I'm not hungry _____ to eat lunch because I ate _____.
3. I never had _____ time to cook, so I eat out often.
4. During my midterm, I study _____, I don't sleep or eat _____.
5. I don't like smoked food because they're _____ salty.

II. Complete the sentences with few, less, little, or fewer.

1. Korean food contains a _____ fat.
2. There is _____ food in the refrigerator.
3. Low fat ice cream has _____ calories.
4. I eat _____ bread every week.
5. I have to eat _____ fat to lose weight.

E LISTENING COMPREHENSION

Listen to the conversation and answer the question.

1. What is the stain on his shirt?
2. How often does he eat this food?
3. Is this food healthy?

F READING COMPREHENSION

Salt, also known as **table salt**, or **rock salt**, is a mineral that is composed primarily of sodium chloride. A little salt is essential for animal life, but too much salt is harmful to animals and plants. Salt is one of the oldest, most ubiquitous food seasonings and salting is an important method for food preservation. The taste of salt (saltiness) is one of the basic human tastes. Salt for human consumption is produced in different forms:

Salt (such as sea salt), refined salt (table salt), and iodized salt. It is a crystalline solid, white, pale pink or light gray in color, normally obtained from sea water or rock deposits. Edible rock salts may be slightly grayish in color because of mineral content.

Source: Wikipedia

Comprehension Questions

Read the paragraph and check the sentences T (true) or F (false).
1. Salt is a mineral composed of chemical stuffs.　　　　　T　F
2. Salt is crucial for animal in proper quantities.　　　　　T　F
3. Salt is used as seasoning.　　　　　　　　　　　　　　T　F
4. Salting is used in traditional food preservation methods.　T　F
5. The taste of salt is not natural for human taste.　　　　T　F

Vocabulary List

ubiquitous : something seems to be everywhere : 어디에나 있는, 아주 흔한
food seasonings : 양념
food preservation : 음식 저장
consumption : the act of buying and using things : 소비
unrefined : in its natural state and has not been processed : 정제되지 않은
iodized salt : 요오드 첨가 식염
crystalline : clear or bright : 수정 같은
deposits : an amount of a substance that has been left somewhere as a result of a chemical or geological process : 침전물
edible : safe to eat and not poisonous : 먹을 수 있는

SENTENCE BUILDING

1. 난 햄버거 같은 패스트푸드는 너무 많이 먹고 과일이나 야채 같은 건강식은 충분히 먹지 않는다.
2. 간식을 너무 많이 먹었기 때문에 난 저녁을 먹을 정도로 배고프지 않아.
3. 공부할 시간이 충분하지 않았기 때문에 시험에서 떨어졌어.
4. 대학에 다니는 동안 공부를 너무 많이 했어. 그래서 잠을 별로 안 자거나 충분히 먹지 못했어.

5. 날생선은 너무 냄새가 나서 좋아하지 않.
6. 한국 음식은 지방이 적다.
7. 우리 집 냉장고에 음식이 조금밖에 안 남아 있다.
8. 난 다이어트를 위해 칼로리를 적게 가진 음식을 먹으려고 노력한다.
9. 난 요즘 탄수화물(carbohydrate/s)을 적게 먹으려고 노력해.
10. 난 다이어트를 위해 지방 섭취를 줄여야 해.

H DISCUSSION

Can you explain why?

The purpose of this discussion is to demonstrate how to give an explanation of something. Please use the key structure in Unit Seven when you debate.

Issue

Can you explain why too much salt is harmful for animals?

Opinion Sample

Although I am not a scientist, I can easily guess why *too much salt* is harmful for animals relating to water. If animals take *too much sodium*, it will lead to the release *too much water* out of their body. Therefore, animals will be dehydrated easily and if water is not supplied into the body soon, the animal may die due to dehydration.

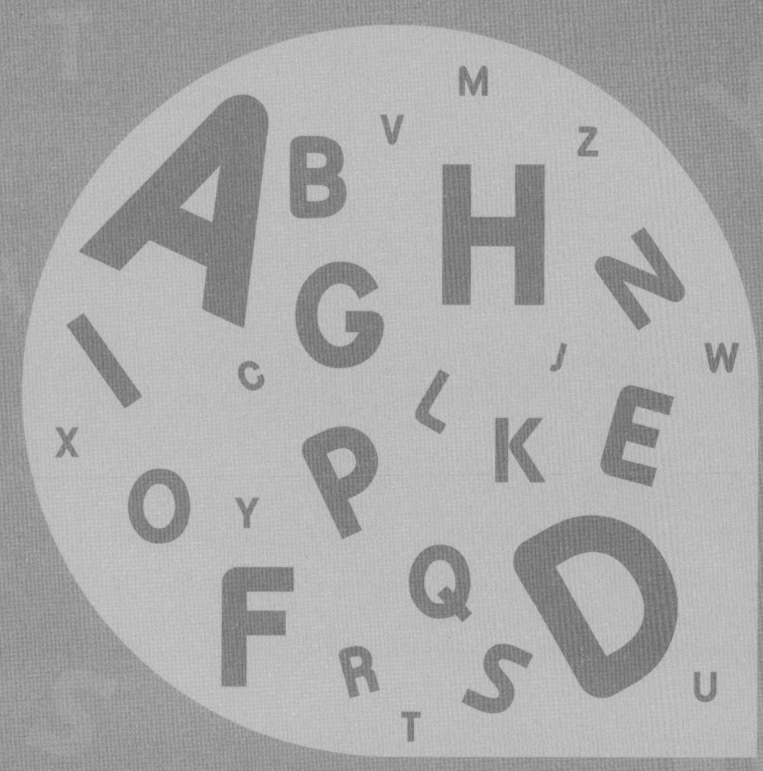

Unit 8 — He is taller than his brother.

A KEY STRUCTURE

- He is taller than his brother.

> Adjective + —er (less than 3 syllable)
> More + adjective (more than 3 syllable)

- **Irregular**
  Good/well → better
  Bad/ill → worse
  Many/much → more

- **Different meaning**
  Old—older—oldest (신구노소)
  　　elder—eldest (혈연관계)
  Late—later—latest (시간)
  　　latter—last (순서)
  Far—farther—farthest (거리)
  　　further—furthest (정도)

B EXTENDED EXPRESSIONS

- **as A as B : B 하려니와 A 하기도 하다**
  She is as shy as foolish.

- **as ~ as ~ can be : 더할 나위 없이 …한**
  She is as happy as she can be.

- **as ~ as one can : 가능한 …한**
  She ran as fast as she could.

- **not so much A as B : A라기보다는 오히려 B다.**
  He is not so much a scholar as a businessman.

- **He has twice as many books as I have.**
  He has two times more books than I have.

- **The 비교급, 비교급 : …하면 …할수록 더 …하다.**
  The more I study, the more questions I have.

- **more A than B : B라기보다는 오히려 A이다.**
  He is more stupid than shy.

- **A is no less B than C is D : C가 D인 거와 마찬가지로 A가 B이다.**
  A whale is no less a mammal than a horse is.

- **not more A than B : B 이상은 A가 아니다. B보다 더 A하지는 않다.**
  He is not smarter than you are.

- **no more than** (= only 단지)
  not more than (= at most 기껏해야)
  no less than (= as much as …만큼이나)
  not less than (= at least 적어도)
  He has no more than 10 bucks.

C SAMPLE DIALOGUE

A: So, you've been in Seoul a year now. What do you think of Seoul?
B: It's great *except for* the weather. [1]
A: Really? I thought the weather is the same as the *Big Apple*. [2]
B: Are you kidding? Seoul is hotter than New York. Seoul is *not so much hot as humid*. [3]
A: I guess it can be pretty bad sometimes.
B: I *used to* live in Utah, but it's dry. [4] It is not as sticky and unpleasant as here. I don't think I'll ever *get used to* it. [5]

> **Note**
> [1] …만 빼고
> [2] Big Apple = New York
> [3] 덥다기보다는 습기가 많다
> [4] …하곤 했다
> [5] 결국 익숙해지다

D PATTERN PRACTICE

> Complete the sentence using the words or phrases in the box. (You may use the same words or phrases again.)

> as, no more than, not so much, no less than, as, than, not more than, more, not less than

1. He has _____ 100 million dollars. He is a true millionaire.
2. She is as high _____ she can be.
3. He typed as fast _____ he could.
4. He is _____ a student as a businessman.
5. The longer I stay, the _____ question I have.
6. He is more stupid _____ innocent.

7. He is _____ a coward.
8. He is _____ six feet tall.
9. He isn't smarter _____ you.
10. He has three times as many clothes _____ I have.

E LISTENING COMPREHENSION

> Karl is calling his friend Eric in Detroit. Complete their conversation using the words and phrases in the box. (There are some extra words.)

> calling, less than, what do you think, as old as,
> no more than, longer, much colder than,
> how do you like, public transportation,
> except for, more, as the same as

A: Hi, Eric, I'm (1) _____ from Detroit.

B: Merry Christmas! (2) _____ Detroit?

A: It's great (3) _____ the weather. It's freezing cold.

B: As far as I know, it's (4) _____ Seoul. So, you don't like the climate! (5) _____ the night life?

A: It is (6) _____ Seoul. Especially, (7) _____ is terrible. It is not easy to live without a car. The nightclubs, Karaoke, and everything else is too far away from my apartment. Detroit is (8) _____ a big city.

B: Seoul has twice the population of Detroit.

A: That's right! Anyway, I miss Seoul. The more I stay, the (9) _____ I miss my home.

B: Did you find some place interesting?

A: Yes, I found a church (10) _____ my great grandfather.

B: Really? That's interesting.

F READING COMPREHENSION

Korean Kids Approach Maximum Possible Height, Weight

The increase in the height and weight of Korean children thanks to better nutrition has slowed down significantly over the past decade.

The Ministry of Education, Science and Technology on Wednesday published the result of a health survey of about 188,000 students from 747 schools nationwide for academic year 2010 which shows that they are up to 6.4cm *taller* and up to 10.54kg heavier *than* their counterparts 20 years ago.

But the average increase in children's height and weight has slowed significantly. For example, the height of an average sixth-grade boy increased 4.79cm between 1980 and 1990, 4cm between 1990 and 2000, and only another 2.15cm between 2000 and 2010.

And the weight of sixth-grade girls increased 4.79kg between 1990 and 2000 but only another 2.65kg over the past decade.

Moon Jin-soo, a professor of children and juvenile medicine at Inje University Ilsan Paik Hospital who analyzed the result of this survey, said, "It seems that the generational change where children have a significantly *better physique than* their parents has now almost stopped." He said the maximum growth possible given the genetic traits of Koreans and the current environment seems to have been reached.

"Average Korean children are already *bigger than* those in other Asian countries like Japan and China," Moon added. "However, there is still room for them to grow *taller* if problems such as lack of sleep, lack of exercise, and nutritional imbalances are resolved."

Source: englishnews@chosun.com Jun. 09, 2011

Comprehension Questions

Read the paragraph and check the sentences T (true) or F (false).
1. The height and weight of Korean children is bigger than what it was a decade ago.   T   F
2. The Korean children are no longer taller and bigger than their parents.   T   F
3. Korean children will still grow taller if problems are solved.   T   F
4. The growth rate has slightly slowed.   T   F
5. Average Korean children are smaller than those in other OECD countries.   T   F

Vocabulary List

nationwide : extending over the whole of a nation : 전국적인
nutrition : the act or process of nourishing : 영양, 영양섭취
significantly : meaning or importance : 의미심장하게
decade : a period of 10 years, a group or series of 10 things, etc. : 10년간, 10편, 10권
counterpart : one of two parts which form a corresponding pair : 상대물, 한 쌍의 한쪽
juvenile : young; youthful : 소년 소녀의, 청소년
physique : the structure of the body with regard to size, shape, proportions and muscular development; the build : 체격, 체형
genetic traits : genetic and environmental factors, personality traits : 유전형질

G   SENTENCE BUILDING

1. 그녀는 바보스럽기도 하려니와 수줍기도 하다.
2. 결혼한 후로 그녀는 더할 나위 없이 행복하다.
3. 그녀는 살기 위해 가능한 빨리 헤엄쳤다.
4. 그는 교수라기보다는 정치인이다.
5. 그는 나보다 2배나 더 많은 돈이 있다.
6. 내가 더 오래 그와 지낼수록 그가 더 좋아진다.
7. 그는 똑똑하기보다는 영리한 편이다.

8. 그가 너보다 더 부자는 아니야.
9. 그는 기껏해야 10불 있어.
10. 그는 적어도 100불 있어.

H DISCUSSION

(Good things and bad things)

The purpose of this discussion is to show both sides of a story. Please use the key structure in Unit Eight when you debate.

(Issue)

What are some good things and some bad things about children having a bigger physique than previous generations?

(Opinion Sample)

When children grow *bigger than* their parents, I think there are *more* positive aspects *than* negative aspects. Bigger and taller children are stronger than small children and being stronger is a good thing. Also being tall is very attractive. One bad thing of being bigger is the increased risk of obesity. Good nutrition doesn't mean over nutrition. However, it tends to increase weight *faster than* height.

Unit 9 What is the tallest mountain in the world?

A KEY STRUCTURE

- The + adjective + −est (less than 3 syllables)
  Who is the tallest in your class?

- The + most/least + adjective (more than 3 syllables)
  Who is the most beautiful woman in history?
  What is the least expensive store?

- Irregular superlatives
  Good → the best
  Bad → the worst
  Who is the best student in your class?
  What is the worst problem in your country?

B EXTENDED EXPRESSIONS

1. Superlative with nouns
   The most + noun
   Which stadium has the most seats?

2. How + adjective−?
   How high is Mount Everest?   It's 8,850 meters high.

C SAMPLE DIALOGUE

A: Welcome to the "What Do You Know" show? Our first contestant is Vanessa. She is from San Francisco, California. Welcome to the show, Vanessa.
B: Thank you. I'm so excited.
A: It's time to play. Are you ready?
B: Yes! Let's play.
A: Here's the first question: What country has the world's tallest building?
B: I know. It's the United Arab Emirates. The world's tallest building is in Dubai.
A: That's correct! The world's tallest building is about 828 meters tall. Good job! Vanessa.

D PATTERN PRACTICE

I. Complete the question using the superlative form of the adjectives or superlative with nouns.

1. What is _____ (large) city?
2. What's _____ (fast) way to travel?
3. Which city has _____ (tourism)?
4. What's _____ (famous) monument?
5. What's _____ (good) university?
6. What's _____ (bad) problem for students?
7. Which airport has _____ (flights) every day?

II. Complete the sentence with the appropriate adjectives from the box. There are some extra words.

> hot, high, wide, large, cold, long, deep, narrow

1. How _____ is the Nile River? It's 6,695 kilometers _____.
2. How _____ is the Grand Canyon? It's about 29 kilometers _____.
3. How _____ is the Sahara Desert? It's 9.1 million square kilometers.

Unit 9 What is the tallest mountain in the world 63

4. How _____ does it get in Death Valley? It can reach 48 degrees Celsius.
5. How _____ is the Pacific Ocean? It's about 11,000 meters _____.

E LISTENING COMPREHENSION

(Listen to the conversation and complete the sentence.)

1. What is the most interesting place you've ever been to?
   Machu Picchu. It's _____.
2. What's the most beautiful place you've seen?
   Monterey Bay has _____.
3. What's the best vacation you've had?
   Bryce Canyon. _____.
4. What's the most exciting thing you've done on a trip?
   I rode _____.
5. What was your worst vacation?
   The Dead horse point was a beautiful canyon but I was _____ and couldn't see or do anything.

F READING COMPREHENSION

(Coba boasts the tallest pyramid on the Yucatán Peninsula)

While still in a poor state of preservation, much of it still unexcavated, the Coba Archaeological Park is notable for its extensive system of ceremonial roads, remote jungle landscape and several interesting pyramids—including the tallest pyramid on the Yucatán Peninsula. Located in the wild eastern half of the Yucatán Peninsula in Mexico, Coba is an hour's drive or bus ride from Tulum.

Comprehension Questions

Read the paragraph and check the sentences T (true) or F (false).
1. Coba is in a good state of preservation.   T   F
2. Coba is famous for the gigantic pyramid.   T   F
3. Coba is located in a tropical forest.   T   F

Vocabulary List

boast : talk about one's achievement very proudly, in a way that other people may find irritating or offensive : 자랑하다

preservation : act that save or protect something from damage or decay : 보존

unexcavated : Not excavated : 발굴되지 않은

　　***excavate** : to dig a hole in the ground, for example in order to build there

archaeological : the study of the societies and peoples of the past by examining the remains of their buildings, tools, and other objects : 고고학의

notable : Someone or something that is notable is important or interesting : 주목할 만한

ceremonial : considered to be representative of an institution, but has very little authority or influence : 의식[예식]의

remote : far away from cities and places where most people live, and are therefore difficult to get to : 떨어진

landscape : everything you can see when you look across an area of land, including hills, rivers, buildings, trees, and plants : 풍경

G SENTENCE BUILDING

1. 요즘 대학생들에게 가장 심각한 문제가 뭡니까?
2. 어떤 도시가 가장 인구가 많나요?
3. 네가 스트레스를 더 많이 받을수록 성적은 더 나빠질 것이다.
　　The 비교급 + 주어 + 동사, the 비교급 + 주어 + 동사
4. 미시시피 강은 얼마나 깁니까?

How + 형용사 + 동사 + 주어

5. 가장 덜 비싼 선물은 무엇이 있을까요?
6. 사촌의 키가 얼마나 되나요?
7. 브라이스 캐니언은 그 아름다움으로 가장 유명하고 약 20킬로미터 폭이다.
8. 나일 강은 6,695킬로미터 길이다.
9. 한국에서 어떤 학교가 학생 수가 가장 많습니까?
10. 사하라 사막에선 얼마나 온도가 올라가나요?

H DISCUSSION

(Which one would you choose?)

Making choices and explain why a certain choice is better than the other. That's the purpose of this discussion. Please use the key structure in Unit Nine when you debate.

(Issue)

Preservation or Development?
Would you preserve the ancient remains as it is or develop the pyramid as a tourist site?

(Opinion Sample)

I think development of ancient remains into a tourist attraction is the better choice. Even if the pyramid were *the tallest and the best* in the world, not many people would visit there and admire its beauty if it is not easy to access. Mexico is a poor country and needs jobs for its people. Developing the cultural relics as tourism sites will help the economy of this country. Of course, responsibility and concerns for environment should be considered.

Unit 10 He is a teacher, isn't he?

A KEY STRUCTURE

- *She is a teacher, isn't she?*
Be 동사가 나오면 부가의문문에서도 그대로 Be 동사를 쓴다.
앞 문장이 긍정이면 부가의문문은 부정

- *He works for a bank, doesn't he?*
일반 동사가 나오면 do/does를 부가의문문으로 쓴다.

- *It's been a while, hasn't it?*
  You're working for Samsung, aren't you?
  He's living in Seoul, isn't he?
축약된 형태는 원래의 동사를 쓴다.

B EXTENDED EXPRESSIONS

- *Let's play tennis, shall we?*
Let's로 시작하는 문장의 부가의문문은 shall we

- *Do it once, will you?*
명령문의 부가의문문은 will you

- *Have a cup of coffee, won't you?*
권유문의 부가의문문은 won't you

- *You'd better go home, hadn't you?*
You'd better로 시작하는 문장의 부가의문문은 hadn't you

- *They used to live there, didn't they?*
동사가 Used to인 문장의 부가의문문은 didn't 주어

C SAMPLE DIALOGUE

A: Hi, Jenifer! *Long time no see*![1]
B: Eli! It's great to see you.
A: *It has been ages*, hasn't it?[2]
B: When was the last time we met?
A: It was Greg's *farewell party*, wasn't it?[3]
B: That's right. *Time flies*.[4]
A: You are still *working for* a bank, aren't you?[5]
B: Not any more! Now I opened my own store.
A: Really! That's great! What a surprise!

Note
[1] 오랜만이다
[2] It has been a while : 꽤 오래됐다, 꽤 시간이 흘렀다
[3] 송별회
[4] 시간 참 빨리 간다
[5] work for/work at : …에 근무하다

D PATTERN PRACTICE

Complete the sentence with tag question.

1. You live in Seoul, _____?
2. He works for Samsung, _____?
3. He is living near Inchon, _____?
4. You're studying English, _____?
5. It has been a long time, _____?
6. Let's dance, _____?
7. Do it now, _____?
8. Have a seat, _____?
9. You'd better go to school, _____?
10. They used to work together, _____?

E LISTENING COMPREHENSION

Listen to the conversation and answer the question.

1. What was the place that has not been changed?
2. When did they used to come to the place?
3. What did they fight over?

F READING COMPREHENSION

Social climbing cuts risk of high blood pressure, doesn't it?

Social climbing could be good for your blood pressure, a study has suggested. Swedish researchers, writing in the Journal of Epidemiology and Community Health, looked at the blood pressure of 12,000 same sex twins and the social status of them and their parents.

Those born with lower socioeconomic status who then moved upwards had lower incidence of high blood pressure than those who remained in a poorer class.

British experts said action was needed to narrow the class gap on health.

High blood pressure (hypertension) is a known risk factor for heart disease and stroke.

But the effect of moving into a higher socioeconomic group was unknown.

One theory says moving into a different social bracket than that of your family and the people you grow up with causes added stress, while another argues that "social climbing" will in itself improve health chances.

In this study, researchers from the Karolinska Institute used data from the Swedish Twin Registry to track adult and parental socioeconomic status among 12,000 same sex twins born between 1926 and 1958.

A postal survey on health and lifestyle was carried out in 1973, and a phone interviews were conducted between 1998 and 2002 as part of the Screening Across the Lifespan Study (SALT).

Questions included any treatment for high blood pressure. Parental occupations were obtained from birth records, which routinely contain this type of information in Sweden.

Source: BBC News Health 12 July 2011

Comprehension Questions

Read the paragraph and check the sentences T (true) or F (false).
1. People who became richer are healthier than those who remain poor.   T   F
2. The research was conducted among same gender twins.   T   F
3. The research used the existing data.   T   F

Vocabulary List

epidemiology : the branch of medical science concerned with the occurrence, transmission, and control of epidemic diseases : 역학(疫學), 전염병학

socioeconomic status : an status, of, relating to, or involving both economic and social factors : 사회 경제적 지위

incidence : The incidence of something bad, such as a disease, is the frequency with which it occurs, or the occasions when it occurs : 발생 정도

stroke : If someone has a stroke, a blood vessel in their brain bursts or becomes blocked, which may kill them or make them unable to move one side of their body : 뇌출혈

registry : a collection of all the official records relating to something, or the place where they are kept : 등록부

G SENTENCE BUILDING

1. 너 파리에 살지, 그렇지?
2. 그녀는 은행에서 일하지, 그렇지?
3. 그는 서울 근처로 이사 오지, 그렇지?
4. 넌 요즘 요가를 연습하지 않니?
5. 3개월이나 됐지, 그렇지?
6. 건배할까요?
7. 당장 내 사무실로 와주지 않을래?
8. 앉으시겠어요?
9. 넌 집에 가는 게 낫겠다, 그렇지?
10. 그들은 학교에 다니곤 했어, 그렇지?

H DISCUSSION

(Is this true?)

The purpose of this discussion is to examine a number of common situations, which people have strong opinions about, to see if they are actually true. Please use the key structure in Unit Ten when you debate.

Issue

I have heard it said that social climbing reduces the risk of high blood pressure. Do you think it is true?

Opinion Sample

It is ridiculous to hear that social climbing reduces the occurrence of high blood pressure, isn't it? In fact, I think it is completely opposite. When a people achieve a higher social status, they usually have gone through many stressful situations. So, it is more likely that the person would have poorer health condition than those who did not have too much stress from the work and social climbing.

Unit 11 I enjoy dancing.

A KEY STRUCTURE

- **S + V + –ing**

  > abandon, give up, quit, admit, allow, permit, enjoy, postpone, defer, delay, put off, avoid, escape, risk, evade, consider, contemplate, appreciate, celebrate, deny, finish, miss, mind, detest, dislike, abominate, advocate

  Meaning: After these verbs, "–ing" form is followed.
  I avoid meeting him.

- **S + V + to + R**

  > afford, appoint, choose, demand, hope, hasten, expect, manage, pretend, refuse, fail, force, plan, decide, determine, threaten, contrive, agree, consent, tend, promise, aid, assist, arrange, ask, claim, defy, desire

  Meaning: After these verbs, "–to + the basic form of verb" is followed.
  I can't afford to buy a car.

- **S + V + to + R / –ing**

  1) Either way is the same meaning

     > attempt, begin, cease, continue, intend, neglect, omit, start, deserve

  2) It has different meaning

     > prefer, like, hate, love, dread, remember, forget, pay, regret, remind

B EXTENDED EXPRESSIONS

1. be afraid to + R 두려워서 …하지 못하다
   be afraid of —ing …하기가 두렵다

2. go on to + R 간헐성 : 계속해서 …하다
   go on —ing 계속성

3. stop to + R …하기 위해서 멈추다
   stop —ing …하는 것을 멈추다

4. mean to + R …할 의도다
   mean —ing …하는 것을 의미하다

5. try to + R …하려고 애쓰다
   try —ing 시험 삼아 …해보다

C SAMPLE DIALOGUE

A: How was your weekend?
B: *I had another wild weekend.* [1]
A: What did you do?
B: You know that I like playing cards. We played cards all night and into the morning. You should come next time.
A: Me? Not really. *I don't like socializing much.* [2] But I enjoy watching *theatrical plays*, although I cannot afford to buy a ticket. [3]
B: Really? I didn't know you had such a good hobby. Let's make a plan to watch a play together!

Note
[1] 정신없는 주말을 보냈어.
[2] 사람들과 어울리는 것을 별로 안 좋아해.
[3] theatrical play : 연극

D PATTERN PRACTICE

(Change the form of the verb and complete the sentence.)

1. I cannot afford _____ out partying when I don't have money. (go)
2. He pretended _____ while his girlfriend talked. (sleep)
3. She gave up _____ because of her health. (smoke)
4. I tried to avoid _____ no. (say)
5. He was trying _____ her; but he ended up scolding her. (help)
6. I prefer _____ by train rather than bus. (travel)
7. I am afraid _____ her the truth because she experienced heart attack before. (tell)
8. I stopped _____ because the doctor told me to. (smoke)
9. I regret not _____ to the Internship Program. (go)
10. My father is afraid _____ me a credit card. (give)

E CLASS ACTIVITY

(Pair Activity)

1. Pair up with your partner.
2. Choose the profession from the list.
3. Make at least three statements using infinitives or gerund about the career value of the profession you choose.
4. Try to guess which profession is being described by your partner.

> social worker, hair designer, plumber, doctor, lawyer
> electrician, fire fighter, carpenter, banker, baker, pastor

(Example)
I like to teach people.

It is important for me to have a lot of research.
I feel satisfaction in doing my work well.
Answer : professor

F LISTENING COMPREHENSION

(Listen to the conversation and answer the question.)

1. What is the problem for the speaker?
2. What is his friend's advice?

G READING COMPREHENSION

(Avoid buying mistakes)

Buying a house? Common mistakes that could scupper your dream deal include overspending, verbal agreements and others.
Making personal comments about a property while in earshot of the seller can knock prospective buyers out of the running, even if they have the financial wherewithal to afford it.

That's the warning from Mike Bester, CEO of Realty International Property Group, who lists this as one of the most common mistakes made by home buyers.

Understanding people's eagerness to upgrade or personalize their new homes, he nevertheless cautions prospective buyers to tone down comments regarding knocking down walls, removing trees or turning the formal lounge into a children's games room while in the presence of sellers. "Sellers are often sentimental about their homes and may become stubborn and difficult to negotiate with if you don't show the necessary respect," says Bester.

Not only is it important to reign in one's emotions to reduce the risk of offending the seller but also in order to remain focused since runaway emotions can cloud judgment and create unreasonable expectations, he adds. "Buyers sometimes become fixated on taking possession of an immaculate property. Realistically, however, they need to accept that there are always going to be repairs or alterations that they will need to take care of if they want to *avoid upsetting* the seller."

Source: Googlenews 30 April 2007

Comprehension Questions

Read the paragraph and check the sentences T (true) or F (false).

1. The most common mistake for home buyers is overspending.   T   F
2. The realty expert advises home sellers not to have verbal agreement before the negotiation.   T   F
3. Home buyers should not give comment regarding alteration of the house in presence of home sellers.   T   F
4. It is important to show respect to home sellers.   T   F
5. Home buyers should not repair their houses after purchase.   T   F

Vocabulary List

scupper : to spoil it completely : 실패하게 하다, 좌절시키다

earshot : If you are within earshot of someone or something, you are close enough to be able to hear them. If you are out of earshot, you are too far away to hear them : 부르면 들리는 거리

prospective : to describe someone who wants to be the thing mentioned or who is likely to be the thing mentioned : 장래의, 유망한

wherewithal : If you have the wherewithal for something, you have the means, especially the money, that you need for it : (무엇을 하는 데 필요한) 돈[수단/기술]

sentimental : relating to or involving feelings such as pity or love, especially for things in the past : (지나치게) 감상적인

stubborn : difficult to remove or to deal with : 없애기[다루기] 힘든, 고질적인

negotiate : talk about a problem or a situation such as a business arrangement in order to solve the problem or complete the arrangement : 협상[교섭]하다

reign : someone or something that reigns supreme is the most important or powerful element in a situation or period of time : 책임 맡는[담당하는] 기간

immaculate : extremely clean, tidy, or neat : 티 하나 없이 깔끔한

H SENTENCE BUILDING

1. 난 내 여자친구에게 비싼 선물을 사줄 수가 없어.
2. 내가 할아버지를 방문했을 때 주무시는 척하셨어.
3. 그는 건강 때문에 일자리 구하는 것을 포기했어.
4. 난 너무 많은 약속을 하는 것을 피하려고 애썼다.
5. 난 그녀를 도우려고 했지만 결국 그녀 인생을 망치고 말았어.
6. 배로 여행하기보다는 비행기로 여행하고 싶어.
7. 그녀를 잃을까 봐 진실을 말하기가 두려워.
8. 의사가 그렇게 하라고 말했기 때문에 운동을 그만뒀어.
9. 지난 겨울에 필리핀에 안 간 걸 후회해.
10. 미국에서 살지 않기로 결정했어.

I DISCUSSION

(What would you do?)

The purpose of this discussion is for you to express your opinion in hypothetical situations. Please use the key structure in Unit Eleven when you debate.

Issue

You lied to your girl friend and if you tell her the truth, she might dump you. What would you do?

Opinion Sample

If I were in that situation, I would tell her the truth no matter what would happen. If I *keep lying* to her, the relationship would not be real. A relationship built on lies will eventually crash. That is 100% certain. If she avoids seeing me for what I did, I have no choice. If she forgives me because I told her the truth, the relationship will *keep going*. So there are 50/50 odds. I will take my chances rather than living a lie.

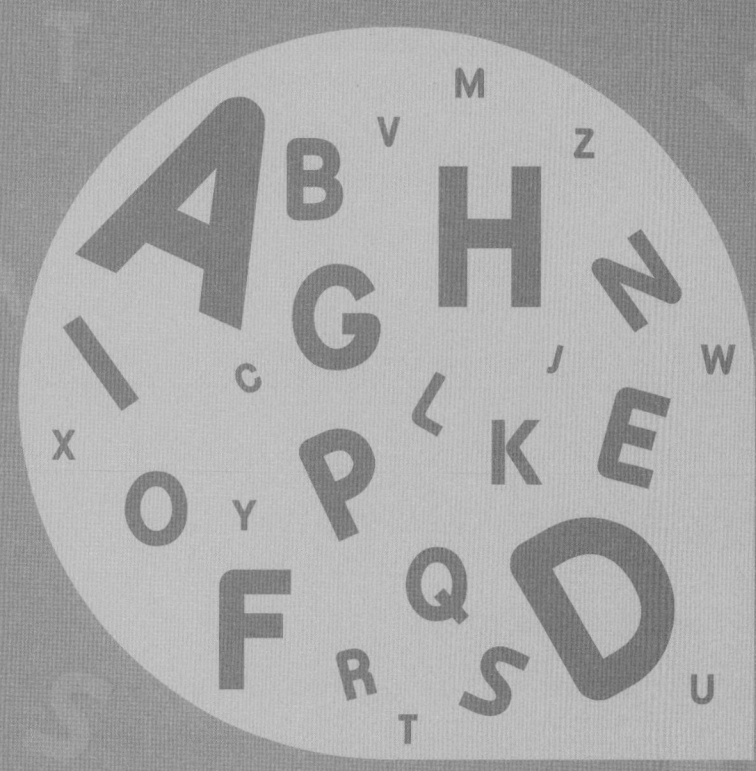

Unit 12 A mouse is chased by a cat.

A KEY STRUCTURE

- S + V + O
  → S + be + p.p. + by + O

  The mouse is chased by a cat.
  능동태의 목적어가 수동태의 주어로 온다.

  He laughed at me.
  → *I was laughed at by him.*
  전치사가 있는 two word verb의 경우 전치사까지 그대로 하나의 동사 취급한다.

  I looked up to her.
  → *She was looked up to by me.*

  He took good care of her.
  → *She was taken good care of by him.*
  → *Good care was taken of her by him.*

  Take good care of는 동사구로 취급해도 되고 take의 목적어인 good care를 목적어로 써도 된다.

B EXTENDED EXPRESSIONS

- I made her a toy.
  → *A toy was made by me (for her).*
  She was made a toy by me. (×)

4형식 문장이며 동사가 다음과 같은 경우 간접 목적어인 her를 주어로 수동태를 만들 수 없다.

> bring, buy, hand, pass, reach, sell, send, throw

- **I kissed her good-bye.**
    → *She was kissed good-bye by me.*

    Good-bye was kissed her by me. (×)

4형식 문장이며 동사가 다음과 같은 경우 직접 목적어인 good-bye가 주어인 수동태를 만들 수 없다.

> answer, call, deny, envy, kiss, refuse, spare

- **She resembled her mother.**
    → Her mother was resembled by her. (×)

> await, let, have, become, cost, resemble

3형식 문장이라 하더라도 동사가 다음과 같은 경우 수동태 문장을 쓸 수 없다.

C SAMPLE DIALOGUE

A: Who painted this picture?
B: It was painted *by* Degas. [1]
A: When was it painted?
B: It was painted *in* 1886. [2]
A: What was it painted with?
B: It was painted *with* oil painting. [3]
A: What was the Thinker sculpted from?
B: It was sculpted *from* bronze. [4]

> Note

수동태 뒤에 전치사 by만 쓰는 것이 아니라 in, with, from 등 다양하게 쓴다.

D PATTERN PRACTICE

(I. Fill in the blank and complete the sentence with the appropriate preposition.)

1. The Sun Flower was painted _____ oil painting.
2. The patient was taken good care _____ by the nurse.
3. The boy was laughed _____ by his classmates.
4. The cave was found _____ 1887.
5. The statue was sculpted _____ stone.

(II. Check the sentence with O if it is correct and X if it is incorrect.)

1. His father was resembled by his son. ( )
2. He was awaited by her girlfriend. ( )
3. I was refused entrance into the club by him. ( )
4. His son was bought a bicycle by his father. ( )
5. She was called good-bye by her boyfriend. ( )

E LISTENING COMPREHENSION

(Listen to the conversation and answer the question.)

1. What are they going to do?
2. Why does her friend tell her not to talk about Martin?

F READING COMPREHENSION

> Thai Opposition Leader Elected Prime Minister

Thailand's parliament *has elected* a new prime minister, Abhisit Vejjajiva, ending a coalition government closely associated with a controversial former prime minister. Protesters battled outside the parliament building after the vote, a sign that the country's deep political divisions remain. Thai opposition leader Abhisit Vejjajiva sits as he attends voting for the Prime Minister at Parliament House in Bangkok, Sep. 12, 2008.
As head of a coalition government, the 44-year-old Mr. Abhisit will be Thailand's 27th prime minister. His election ends a year of government by parties aligned with former Prime Minister Thaksin Shinawatra.

Many Thais hope Monday's vote will end months of political tensions. Those tensions *were worsened* when thousands of anti-government demonstrators laid siege to the prime minister's office building and then blockaded Bangkok's airports earlier this month.

Sompob Manarangsan, an economics professor at Chulalongkorn University, says the vote will help restore confidence in Thailand's democracy.

Source: englishnews@chosun.com December 16, 2008

> Comprehension Questions

Read the paragraph and check the sentences T (true) or F (false).

1. The government succeeded the election and the head of the previous government became the prime minister.   T   F
2. There were political divisions and demonstrations before the election.   T   F
3. The vote contributes to regain Thailand's democracy.   T   F

Vocabulary List

coalition : a combination or temporary alliance, especially between political parties : 합동, 연합
controversial : usually long-standing dispute or argument, especially one where there is a strong difference of opinion : 토론의, 논쟁상의
parliament : the highest law-making assembly of a nation : 의회, 국회
political divisions : 정치적 양분화
aligned : to put something in a straight line or bring it into line : …을 일렬로 하다
siege : the act or process of surrounding a fort or town with troops, cutting off its supplies and subjecting it to persistent attack with the intention of forcing its surrender : 포위, 공략

G SENTENCE BUILDING

1. 황소라는 그림은 유화로 그려졌다.
2. 그의 아내에 의해 그는 보살핌을 잘 받는다.
3. 그 소년은 반 친구들이 비웃었기 때문에 화가 났다.
4. 그녀의 남자친구로부터 그녀를 위한 꽃이 생일 선물로 주어졌다.
5. 핵폭탄은 1945년도에 사용되었다.
6. 생각하는 사람은 동으로 만들어졌다.
7. 아버지에 의해 아들을 위한 공이 던져졌다.
8. 그녀는 이민국 직원에 의해 미국으로의 입국이 거절당했다.
9. 우리집에서 제일 비싼 가구가 나에 의해 이웃에게 팔렸다.
10. 시간이 지날수록/세월이 갈수록 괴물이 되어 간다.

H DISCUSSION

(What is the difference?)

The purpose of this discussion is to show how to make distinctions between opposites. Please use the key structure in Unit Twelve when you debate.

(Issue)

What is the difference between democracy and dictatorship?

(Opinion Sample)

The major difference between democracy and dictatorship is whether or not the public opinions *are reflected* in decision-making process. In simple terms, democracy is government for the majority by the majority. However, dictatorships do not have to be responsible to the people because their power is not based on the consent of a majority. Democratic societies usually have more freedom and rights than societies living under dictatorships. One good example of a democracy is South Korea. A good example of a dictatorship is North Korea. In South Korea, people elect their leaders and have the right to free speech but in North Korea people can not elect their leaders and do not have the right to free speech. Therefore in the South Korean example of democracy, the people have the right to make decisions in political decisions but in the North Korean example of dictatorship people do not have the right to have their opinion represented in political decisions.

Unit 13 He must be his father.

A KEY STRUCTURE

- **cannot be ↔ must be**
  She cannot be her mother. …일 리 없다
  She must be her mother. …임에 틀림없다

- **It + be + adjective + that + S + (should) + R**
  = It + be + adjective + of + O + to + R

  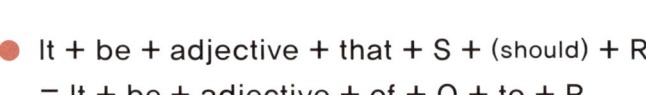
  kind, wise, polite, rude, stupid, careful, sorry,
  convenient, necessary, important, difficult

  It is important that she should follow the format.
  = It is important of her to follow the format.

- **require, insist, order, suggest, desire, advise, decide + that + S + (should) + R**
  The general ordered that every soldier should obey the rule.

B EXTENDED EXPRESSIONS

- **used to + R** – 과거의 규칙적인 습관
  I used to get up early in the morning.
  be used to (= be accustomed to) **+ ~ing/N** …하는 데 익숙해 있다.
  He was used to being humiliated.

- **had better + R** ···하는 편이 났다.
  would better + R
  I had better go now.

C SAMPLE DIALOGUE

A: Do you think you're a healthy person?
B: Yes, I do. I hardly ever get sick. But I used to have a cough all the time.
A: Really? How did you overcome your health problem?
B: Whenever I have a health problem, I try to take my grandmother's *remedy*.[1] Following natural treatments is very important to me. But it requires me to be patient.
A: It is O.K. to take time. I think you'd better follow *natural therapy*.[2] I suggest that you watch a health and medicine TV program. It gives you lots of *common sense* tips about staying healthy.[3]
B: It is very kind of you to give me such useful advice. *I will keep it in my mind*.[4]

Note
[1] 요법
[2] 민간요법
[3] 상식
[4] 명심할게

D PATTERN PRACTICE

Find the appropriate word in the box and complete the conversation or sentence.

> of, must be, take, had better, stupid,
> should, obey, used to, cannot be, am used to

1. A: Linda is wearing a tank top today.
   B: That woman _____ Linda. She never wears a such clothing.
2. A: Look at this picture. Michelle and this woman look alike.
   B: She _____ Michelle's sister.
3. A: I have been doing a part-time job.
   B: I _____ do a part-time job too.
4. A: I _____ being teased.
   B: If someone teases you, I will punish him or her.
5. A: I sat up all night playing computer games.
   B: You _____ sell the computer. It hurts your health.
6. The doctor suggested that I _____ take the pill every day.
7. It is very kind _____ you to show me the way.
8. It is important that all students _____ the rule.
9. He insists that we _____ a train instead of driving a car.
10. It was _____ of me to believe the rumor.

E LISTENING COMPREHENSION

Listen to the conversation and answer the question.

1. What is the problem?
2. Why can't he take the day off?
3. What does his friend think is the cause of the headache?
4. How long does the pain last?
5. What is his friend's advice?

F READING COMPREHENSION

> Korea Prepared for Aging Population

Korea's population is aging faster than any other country, but it *must be* one of the worst prepared nations to deal with the impact of this worrying trend. According to a study by the Center for Strategic and International Studies, a U.S. foreign policy think tank, Korea ranked 19th out of 20 countries surveyed in terms of its Income Adequacy Index, the Ministry of Strategy and Finance said on Sunday.

The survey used two indexes — Income Adequacy and Fiscal Sustainability. *It is important of each country to try and gauge* how well prepared to deal with its aging population.

Korea finished almost bottom of the list, one spot behind China and one ahead of Mexico. It only fared slightly better in the fiscal sustainability index, where it placed 12th. This index "takes into account the differing fiscal room that countries have to accommodate their growing old-age dependency burdens," the CSIS said.

Korea now finds itself in the same position as France and Italy, which also ranked poorly in both categories. These countries are struggling with a need to tap into their state funds to aid senior citizens who are not earning enough to support themselves, but are hobbled at present by their respective fiscal limitations.

CSIS has advised Korea to boost its pension fund savings and bolster its social safety net to support senior citizens with financial troubles, while increasing the birthrate and allowing more people to immigrate to the country.

Source: modified from english news@chosun.com Jul. 18, 2011

> Comprehension Questions

Read the paragraph and check the sentences T (true) or F (false).

1. A high percent of Korean population are senior citizens.   T F
2. Korea is well prepared to deal with the impact of an aging society.   T F
3. Mexico is a better country in terms of preparing pension funds for old people.   T F
4. Korea ranked as the same as France and Italy in fiscal sustainability index.   T F
5. Increasing the birthrate and immigration rate will resolve the current problem.   T F

Vocabulary List

Income Adequacy Index : 수입 적합 지표

fiscal : belonging or relating to government finances or revenue : 국고의, 재정의

sustainability : capable of being sustained : 지속(유지)가능성

accommodate : to provide someone with a place in which to stay : 수용하다, 적합하다, 돌보다, 공급하다

hob : the flat surface on which pots are heated, either on top of a cooker or as a separate piece of equipment : 요리판

coffers : a large chest for holding valuables : 상자, 금고

senior citizens : 노인

equate : to be equivalent to it : 동등하게 나타내다, 균등하게 하다

boost : to improve or encourage something or someone : …을 밀어올리다, 격려하다, 후원하다

pension : a government allowance to a retired, disabled or widowed person : 연금

bolster : to support it, make it stronger or hold it up : 베개받이, 받침

social safety net : 사회 안전망

birthrate : 출산율

G SENTENCE BUILDING

1. 제인이 그녀의 동생일 리가 없어. 제인이 그녀보다 훨씬 나이 들어 보여.
2. 그녀가 엄마일 거야, 크리스티나는 엄마를 닮았어.

3. 그렇게 말하다니 너는 참 공손하구나.
4. 선생님은 모든 학생들이 그의 방법을 따라야 한다고 주장했다.
5. 난 아침에 아침식사를 거르곤 했다.
6. 그는 비웃음을 당하는 것에 익숙했다.
7. 난 숙제를 나중에 하는 것보다 지금 하는 편이 나아.
8. 그가 일자리에 되도록 많이 지원하는 것이 필요하다.
9. 그가 그녀의 이야기를 믿다니 어리석군.
10. 규칙을 바꾸는 것은 그에게 편리하다.

H DISCUSSION

What would happen if – ?

The purpose of this discussion is to explain what is likely to happen under certain circumstances when the circumstance brought unexpected results. Please use the key structure in Unit Thirteen when you debate.

Issue

What would happen if the birthrate were too low?

Opinion Sample

If the birthrate were too low, the number of children will decrease. There will be many consequences from a low birthrate. First, *it is necessary that many schools be closed*. Since the number of newcomers will reduce, some schools will not need to be open. Second, when the children grow up, many companies will have a hard time to find employees. Job seekers can ask for raises and move between jobs any time they want. The production rate will be decreased because of it. Third, there will be more elderly people than young people. Young people will have to make more money to support their parents.

Unit 14 The man looking at the map is a tourist.

A KEY STRUCTURE

- **Modify noun before or after the noun**

  The wounded soldier went to a hospital.
  Don't wake up a sleeping baby.
  The man looking at a map is a tourist.

  분사는 동사를 형용사의 기능을 갖게 해주는 것인데 명사 앞이나 뒤에서 수식한다.

  어떤 경우에 현재부사를 쓰고 어떤 경우에 과거분사를 쓰는가?
  Vi : ~ing (진행 : …하고 있는)
  　　 ~ed (완료 : …해버린)
  　　A dancing queen, a sleeping baby
  　　Fallen leaves, retired employee

  Vt : ~ing (능동/사역 : …시키는)
  　　 ~ed (수동 : …된, …당한)
  　　A wounded student, a broken window
  　　An exciting game, a boring person

  자동사의 경우 "…하고 있는" 또는 "…해버린" 의 뜻을 가진다.
  타동사의 경우 "…시키는" 또는 "…된" 의 뜻을 가진다.

- **감정동사의 경우 명사를 수식할 때는 현재분사를 쓰고, 사람이 주어로 쓰이면 과거분사를 쓴다.**

  I watched an exciting game.
  I was excited by watching the game.

- S + V + C
  S + V + O + O.C

  This book is very interesting.
  I saw him crossing the street.

  2형식이나 5형식 문장에서 보어로 분사가 쓰인다.

B EXTENDED EXPRESSIONS

Frankly speaking, she is a foolish woman.
→ *If we speak frankly, I will tell you she is a foolish woman.*

분사구문은 접속사, 주어가 생략된 형태임.

C SAMPLE DIALOGUE

A: Hey, Catherine. How are you doing?

B: I am bored.

A: Do you want to go bowling with us on Friday night?

B: Bowling is boring.

A: I bet it won't be boring. Do you know who is coming?

B: I have no idea. Are *celebrities* coming to the bowling center?[1]

A: Yes, how did you know? The actor in the movie "Batman" is coming there to *shoot for a film.*[2]

B: Oh, my God! I can't believe this. I am so excited. I am a huge fan of his!

A: See, I told you.

> **Note**
> [1] celebrity : 연예인
> [2] 영화 찍다

D PATTERN PRACTICE

> Read the sentence and complete the sentence with the proper form.

1. I like the girl _____ a book in a bench. (read)
2. I saw the boy _____ a big straw hat. (wear)
3. I am so _____ to meet my friend. (excite)
4. I watched the _____ game on TV last night. (excite)
5. I was _____ by the sad story. (touch)
6. He saw the dog _____ by the window. (bark)
7. A short- _____ dog greeted me at the entrance. (tail)
8. I was _____ at the news. (disappoint)
9. She is good at soothing a _____ baby. (cry)
10. She collected the _____ leaves in her book. (color)

E LISTENING COMPREHENSION

> Listen to the conversation and answer the question.

1. What is the plan for the speaker on the weekend?
2. What is the reason for his plan?
3. What is the reason his friend cannot join?
4. What does he ask for his friend?

F READING COMPREHENSION

N. Korean Military's Morale 'Weakening'

An increasing number of North Korean military officers and soldiers are caught *watching* South Korean films or soap operas in barracks, sources say.

A Beijing-based source who visits the North often said Monday, "Several Army officers and soldiers have been caught *watching* South Korean movies or TV dramas since last year, and the military has been providing extensive indoctrination for all officers and soldiers with a view to preventing the cultural infiltration of imperialism."

The North Korean military's discipline and morale are eroding under international sanctions, with one officer caught selling DVDs in the North Korea-China border region.
The poor state of military discipline is due mainly to economic difficulties since the botched currency reform in late 2009. The food shortage is worsening in barracks, as it has become difficult to collect food from the public.

A Beijing-based Chinese North Korea expert said, "It's likely that the North Korean military's power to distribute resources has weakened as the regime shifted its priority from the military to the party after the big party congress last year."

Source: englishnews@chosun.com / Jul. 06, 2011

Comprehension Questions

Read the paragraph and check the sentences T (true) or F (false).

1. Despite severe punishment, more military personnel watch Korean Dramas. T   F
2. N. Korea prohibits watching Korean dramas to prevent the cultural influence. T   F
3. The reason for weakening discipline is because of economic difficulties. T   F

4. The success of the currency reform contributes to the eroding of morale.　　T　F

5. The military's power has weakened as the regime shifted.　　T　F

Vocabulary List

soap operas : 연속극 드라마
barracks : building or group of buildings for housing soldiers : 군대 막사
extensive : large in area, amount, range or effect : 광범위한, 광대한, 넓은
indoctrination : 교화, 개발
infiltration : act of filling or closing gaps, holes, etc. : 침입, 침투
imperialism : the power of, or rule by, an emperor or empress : 제국주의, 영토확장주의
discipline : strict training, or the enforcing of rules, intended to produce ordered and controlled behavior in oneself or others : 훈련, 단련, 수양
morale : the level of confidence or optimism in a person or group; spirits : 사기, 의기, 패기
erode : to wear away, destroy or be destroyed gradually : …을 서서히 파괴하다
sanction : official permission or authority : 허가, 인가
botched : to repair something carelessly or badly : …을 망쳐놓다
currency reform : 화폐개혁
regime : a system of government : 정권
big party congress : 전당대회

G   SENTENCE BUILDING

1. 책을 읽고 있는 남자가 이 학교 교장 선생님이시다.
2. 상처 입은 환자가 병원에서 간호사에 의해 보살핌을 받는다.
3. 난 그녀가 사거리에서 길을 건너고 있는 것을 보았다.
4. 난 게임이 재미있을 거라 생각했었는데 지루했다.
5. 잠자고 있는 아이를 깨우지 마라.
6. 은퇴한 사람들을 위해서 세금이 감면되어야 한다.
7. 정오까지 깨진 창문을 고쳐 놓을게.

8. 솔직히 말하자면 그는 현명한 사람이 아니다.
9. 난 그녀가 파티에서 빨간 드레스를 입고 있는 것을 보았어.
10. 지난 주말에 흥미 있는 TV 프로그램을 시청했어.

H DISCUSSION

What has this change brought?

The purpose of this discussion is to look deeply at how one kind of change led to other change. Please use the key structure in Unit Fourteen when you debate.

Issue

If the Korean peninsula is reunited, what has this change brought?

Opinion Sample

If Korea becomes a *united nation*, Korea might be changed greatly in many aspects. First, the economy will grow dramatically because *Korea will not be the country spending much money for military purposes*. It is true that a big portion of the annual budget has been spent on the military; however, after unification we can focus on economic development. Second, Korea will no longer be a small country. Since North Korean population will be added and territory will become larger, the geographical and demographic makeup of Korea will be changed. Third, the language will be changed. Since North Korea has its unique language heritage, the influence from North Korean language will be big or vice versa.

Script & Answer Keys

Unit 1

Pattern practice answers

1. Have you ever lost your wallet?
2. Have you ever seen a light bug?
3. Have you ever eaten weird foods?
4. Have you ever spoken to a celebrity?
5. Have you ever tried climbing?
6. Have you ever fallen asleep in the subway?
7. Have you ever drunk hard liquor all night?
8. Have you ever hit a child?
9. Have you ever had your heart broken?
10. Have you ever slept at a friend's house?
11. Have you ever won a medal?
12. Have you ever kissed a girl?
13. Have you ever shaven your head?
14. Have you ever forgotten a meeting?

Audio script

A: Hi! Amy! How're you doing?
B: Oh, I don't know. Not so good, I guess.
A: Really? What's the matter?
B: It's my boyfriend. I forgot his birthday and now he won't talk to me.
A: That's too bad. Have you called him to apologize?
B: Well, I've tried to call, but he doesn't answer the phone.
A: Hmm, have you e-mailed him?
B: No, I haven't yet, but maybe I should.
A: And maybe you should send him a romantic "I am sorry" card.
B: Mmm, yeah, that might help.
A: And why don't you give him a bottle of nice aftershave or cologne?
B: Hey, that's not a bad idea.
A: Yep, that usually works for me. Oh, and one more good idea.
B: Uh huh, what's that?
A: You'd better write down his birthday on your calendar.
B: Definitely! Well, thanks for the suggestions.
A: No problem. Let me know what happens.

Listening comprehension answers

1. call
2. i) send a romantic "I am sorry" card
   ii) give presents such as aftershave or cologne
3. write down her boyfriend's birthday on her calendar

Reading comprehension

I have been to Mexico.

난 여러 번 멕시코에 가본 적이 있다. 우리 할머니가 멕시코에 계셔서 어버이날과 크리스마스에 거의 매번 방문하곤 했다. 할머니 댁에 가는 것은 굉장히 좋은 경험이었기 때문에 갈 때마다 우리는 무척 재미있었다. 할머니 댁 근처에는 우리가 뛰어놀고 게임을 할 수 있는 오래된 농장이 있었다. 그 추억들을 돌이켜 보면 그 오래된 농장에서 놀 때만큼 나의 상상력이 활동적이었을 때가 없었던 것 같다. 우리는 닭과 개를 쫓으면서 온 곳을 헤집고 다녔다. 나와 내 자매들은 우리가 동물들에게 사료를 주는 농부인 척하며 들에서 뛰어놀았다. 지금 생각해보면 나는 내 인생에서 꽤 많은 여행을 했다. 난 학교 현장학습으로 보스턴, 뉴욕, 워싱턴에 가본 적이 있다. 각각의 여행은 재미있었지만 그 어떤 것도 멕시코에서 할머니 댁에 갔던 여행과는 비교할 수 없다. 난 라스베이거스에 수없이 가봤다. 나는 대학생 때 라스베이거스에서 2시간 정도 떨어진 곳에 살아서 나와 내 친구들은 쇼를 보기 위해서나 아니면 단순히 길거리에서 파는 유명한 핫도그를 먹기 위해 거의 주말마다 그곳에 갔다. 가끔 우리는 라스베이거스에서 너무 재미있게 놀아서 월요일이 돌아오면 흥분을 가라앉히고 공부하는 일상으로 돌아오는 게 어려웠다.

Reading comprehension answers

1. He has visited Mexico to visit his grandma who used to live there.

2. He has visited there for a school field trip.

3. He lived only 2 hours away from Las Vegas.

Sentence building

1. My professor wrote the English grammar book for college students last winter.

2. My brother learned high level of computer program at a private institute last February.

3. I have learned Taekwondo for 10 years.

4. I have learned English for last 12 years.

5. I have studied English in an English-speaking country.

6. I have practiced ballet in France.

7. I have taken advanced level of computer classes at the Engineering School.

8. I have acquired the Barista certificate when I was in the United States.

9. I have visited Jeju Island for school field trip.

10. I have visited Washington D.C. while I studied in New York.

Unit 2

Pattern practice answers

1. type   2. to wash   3. clean   4. altered   5. playing
6. robbed 7. yell   8. stolen   9. come   10. speak

Audio script

A: So what's new with you? Are you still working for a software company?

B: No, not any more. They made me copy other companies' products. So I quit and started my own business.

A: That's great! Are you still swimming a lot?

B: No, not so much any more. I broke my legs last year.

A: That's too bad.

B: Now I am really into yoga instead.

A: Sounds like fun. Hey, do you still see any of our old friends?

B: Well, I see Tony a lot.

A: Really? I haven't seen him in ages. He works for Samsung, doesn't he?

B: Uh, not any more. Now he works for my software company.

A: Really? So do you make him copy the same software that the other companies make?

B: No way! I had him create a brand new game program. It will be a big hit.

A: O.K. Good luck!

Listening comprehension answers

	Job	Exercise	Friend
Old	Software company	swimming	Samsung
Current	His own software company	yoga	Software company

Reading comprehension

김 씨는 중독의 악마와 공개적 망신으로부터 자신의 직업과 개인 생활의 기쁨을 되찾기 위해 싸웠다. 김 씨는 1998년 대종상을 수상하였고 2001년에는 칸 국제 영화제에 남우주연상 후보로 지명되기도 했다. 그러나 그것은 어린 시절부터 가족농장에서 열심히 일하는 것을 배운 사람에게조차 아주 힘든 여정이었다. 48세인 김 씨는 "저는 아름답게 끝난 작품을 보는 것을 좋아합니다."라고 말했다. 그리고 "아직도 연기력을 향상시키기 위해 제 연기를 모니터합니다. 매번 다른 역할을 맡을 때마다 너무 신이 나요."라고 손뼉을 치며 말했다. "팬들이 행복해 하고 그들이 내 영화를 보는 것이 제게는 즐거움입니다. 팬들이 제 인생을 바꾸도록 했습니다. 인생이 항상 즐거운 것만은 아닙니다."라고 그는 말했다.

Reading comprehension answers

1. An actor

2. He won the Dajongsang Film Award and nominated for the candidate at the Cannes Film Festival.

3. He used to have drug addiction but overcame the problem. Now he can help others.

Sentence building

1. I had my boyfriend do my English homework.
2. I have my car fixed by next Friday.
3. I asked my husband to drop off our daughter at the kindergarten.
4. I got my teacher to put off the test until the end of the semester.
5. My school requires me to attend the chapel once in every week.
6. I saw my girlfriend playing the piano.
7. I helped my father (to) fix the roof.
8. My family saw him beaten by robbers.
9. Although I heard my sister yell at me, I did not even respond.
10. I had my backpack stolen in a crowded bus.

Unit 3

Pattern practice answers

1. I have a friend who/that calls me a lot to talk about her boyfriend.
2. I made some new friends at a hobby club which/that organizes hiking trips.
3. My best friend has a guitar that/which she bought from a singer.
4. I know someone who/that throws a big party once a year.
5. I have a really interesting friend who(m)/that I met at my college.
6. I found the cool Web site that/which helps you to find your old friends.
7. Carolina is someone who(m)/that I can trust.

* 현대 영어에서는 대명사 목적격 대신 주격으로 대신하는 경우가 많습니다.

8. Nina is a woman whose son is a rebel.
9. Jenny talks about the things that/which she is doing.
10. She had a company that/which planned weddings.

Audio script

I always look forward to seeing the clerk who works at a café.

I always drink coffee at the café after lunch. The coffee shop is really busy, you know, and she gets stressed out. She is very friendly, though. She always says, "Good afternoon. How are you today?" It's nice to hear a friendly voice every day.

Another person I enjoy seeing is my computer teacher. I am taking a class in Web design, and we're learning to make our own Web sites. Anyway, the teacher is really nice. He is kind of demanding, though. I mean, he always gives us a lot of homework. But, I really look forward to his class. He makes the class fun.

Then there's my yoga instructor. She's incredibly easygoing. She can be a bit strict, though. I mean. She likes to start class on time, and she doesn't like people to come to class late. But she's really good at explaining how to do yoga.

Listening comprehension answers

1. friendly   2. demanding   3. strict

Reading comprehension

7살짜리 소녀가 캘리포니아 세크라멘토에서 큰 십자가가 떨어져 머리를 부딪혀 사망했다. 경찰은 구체적인 사망원인을 아직 밝혀내지 못했지만 소녀가 교회에서 십자가를 옮기려다 사망한 것으로 추정한다. 지방뉴스에 따르면 소녀는 그 끔찍한 사건이 일어났을 때 다른 형제 두 명과 함께 있었고 어머니는 당시 현장에 없었다. 소녀의 형제들은 오후 2시경 그 사건이 일어났을 때 끔찍한 사고현장에 함께 있었다.

그 가족을 잘 아는 다른 교구인이 자신은 그러한 일이 무고한 소녀에게 일어난 것에 대해 매우 화가 난다고 기자에게 말했다.

Reading comprehension answers

1. The girl was trying to move the cross and a large cross fell off and hit her head.
2. The girl was at the church with two other siblings.

Sentence building

1. I have a friend who calls me late at night.
2. I met some people at a meeting which/that organizes overseas travel.
3. My friend has a book on which he got a signature from the author.
4. I know a guy who/that throws a big birthday party for his girlfriend.
5. I have a really interesting friend who/that I met in my English class.
6. I found the agency that/which helps me to find my job.
7. My mother is the one whom I can trust at any circumstances.
8. I know a girl whose brother is a rebel.
9. My friend talks about the part time job that/which s/he is doing every time I meet him/her.
10. She goes a company that/which supports education for its employees.

Unit 4

Pattern practice answers

1. met 2. been 3. gotten 4. made 5. asked
6. answered 7. come 8. be 9. have 10. studied

Audio script

This is a long weekend and Lisa has three days off. She decides to go on vacation. She searched the Internet and found some good deals on flights to Orlando, Florida. She could get a round trip ticket for $324. However, *if she had reserved her flight seven days ahead, she might have purchased the ticket for $256*. The flight takes an hour and half. It leaves at 1:00 p.m. on Friday and the return flight leaves Orlando, Florida at 10:00 a.m. on Sunday. The hotel costs $150 a night plus tax and service charge, which is $19.50 per night. After she purchased the airplane ticket, she accidently found out that train will take only four hours. The train leaves at 8:00 a.m. on Friday and the return train leaves Orlando, Florida at 7:00 p.m. on Saturday. She does not need to reserve a hotel room for two nights. The train costs $235, but she can stay just one night and still have one day for resting. Of course, she can have two full days of sightseeing. *If she traveled by train, it would save a lot of money. Or if she had reserved her flight earlier, she might have saved some money.* She learns a lesson that travel requires planning in advance.

Listening comprehension answers

	Cost of transportation	Cost of lodging	Total cost
By plane	$324	($150×2) + ($19.50×2)	663
By plain a week ahead	$256	($150×2) + ($19.50×2)	635
By train	$235	$150 + $19.50	404.5

Reading comprehension

난 15년 동안 인디애나에서 편의점을 운영해왔다. 한 친구는 죽임을 당했고 다른 한 가게 주인은 무장강도에 의해 심하게 권총으로 맞아 부상을 당했다. 편의점에서 무장강도를 당하는 일은 꽤 흔하다. 우리는 뉴스에 나온 사건에서 만약 젊은 가게 점원이 총을 발사하지 않았더라면 강도가 무슨 짓을 했을지 아무도 모른다. 점원은 아직도 심장이 벌떡거리면서 강도 사건 직후 인터뷰를 했다. 그는 그 상황에서 그가 해야 될 일을 했을 뿐이라고 말했다. 만약 점원이 강도를 쏘지 않았더라면 강도가 가게에 있는 누군가를 쏘았을까? 우리는 절대 알 수가 없다. 그러나 무장강도를 쏘았다고 해서 그 사람에게 살인죄를 부과하는 것은 옳지 않다. 만약 젊은 가게 점원이 총을 발사하지 않았더라면 비록 무장강도가 가게에서 아무도 쏘지 않았다고 하더라도 누군가는 죽을 수도 있었다. 난 법원의 결정에 대해 부끄럽게 생각한다.

Reading comprehension answers

1. A young store clerk shot the armed robber before he attacked.
2. He thinks it is not fair to convict murder for the store clerk even though the armed robber did not attack anyone in the store.

Sentence building

1. If I had had the part time job experiences, I would have been selected for the Intern of the company.
2. If I had arrived at the school earlier, I could have taken the English class.
3. He would have gotten along well with his friends, if he had been friendly.
4. If I had joined the study group, I would be abroad now.
5. I would fall asleep now if I would have not taken too much coffee.
6. I wish I had gone to the Himalaya Mountain.
7. He treats me as if I were a maid.
8. I felt so comfortable to be with her as if we had talked before.
9. If I had been in your shoes, I would have dropped off the wallet at the police station.
10. I wish I were Superman.

Unit 5

Pattern practice answers

1. I have been seeing my boyfriend lately.
2. I have been watching movies lately.
3. I have been eating out lately.
4. I have been listening to music lately.
5. I have been taking a nap lately.
6. I have been surfing Internet lately.
7. I have been doing part time job lately.
8. I have been studying English lately.
9. I have been being on a blind date lately.
10. I have been going to a pottery class lately.
11. I have been spending time with my family lately.
12. I have been doing exercise lately.
13. I have been watching TV shows lately.
14. I have been traveling Europe lately.
15. I have been practicing Taekwondo lately.
16. I have been working late lately.
17. I have been taking classes lately.
18. I have been playing golf lately.

Audio script

A: Have you ever seen Ringling Bros. Circus? I've just been reading about their new show.

B: No, I don't think so. What is -uh-?

A: It's an American circus group. They are basically a group of entertainers started from the 19th century. The performers came from all over the world. Look, here's a picture.

B: Oh, I see. Jenny has been talking about this circus all this week. I have heard that it's really amazing.

A: Yeah! Totally. Listen to this review. "Ringling Bros. Circus has performed in more than 130 cities around the world."

B: I think I saw something about them on TV. What else

does the review say?

A: Well, this is interesting. It says that Ringling Bros. Circus perform with animals but it has elephant conservation center.

B: That is amazing. They do care about animals. Have you ever seen them perform?

A: Yes, I have. I saw one of their shows about three years ago. I'd really recommend it.

B: I think we should go. How long has the new show been performing in town?

A: It has been performing for three weeks. I'm going to go online to find out about tickets.

B: That's a good idea!

Listening comprehension answers

1. F 2. T 3. T
4. F 5. T 6. F

Reading comprehension

음식은 당신이 어디로부터 왔는지 또 어떤 교훈을 얻었는지에 대해 많을 것을 말해줍니다. 음식은 지리학, 정치학, 전통, 믿음과 그 이상 많은 것을 의미합니다. 김이 모락모락 나는 비빔밥을 앞에 두고 앉아서 캐서린 김 씨는 음식에 관한 아버지의 가장 중요한 규칙을 회상합니다. 그녀의 아버지는 음식이 따뜻할 때 제공되지 않으면 잘 먹은 것 같지 않다고 했습니다. 그녀는 김이 나는 밥그릇에 젓가락으로 밥을 떠서 식기를 기다리곤 했다고 회상합니다. 뜨거운 음식과 더불어 아주 매운 맛은 교포 1세대를 특징짓는 한국 요리법의 주성분입니다. 아마도 김 씨의 마음은 그녀의 가족의 전통과 연결되어 있지만 그녀의 입맛은 거의 평생동안 미국에서 길들여져 왔습니다. "저는 최근 한국 음식을 어떻게 조리하는지 배워오고 있는데, 그것은 나의 어린 시절을 상기시켜주고 나와 부모님 세대에 다리를 놓아주기 때문입니다. 제가 나이가 들수록 한국 음식이 좋아지고 한국 음식을 먹으면 고향에 있는 것처럼 느껴집니다."라고 세 살 때 전 가족이 미국으로 이민한 김 씨가 말했습니다.

Reading comprehension answers

1. Serve while it's hot and spicy taste
2. The Korean food reminds her of her childhood.
   The Korean food brides her and her parents' generation.

Sentence building

1. He have been being on a date with a girl who graduated the same high school with him.
2. I have been learning Takwondo for the last 10 years/the last decade.
3. How long have you been lived in the U.S.A.?
4. How long have you been doing yoga?
5. How long have you been taking English classes?
6. How often have you been taking English conversation classes?
7. I have been watching video clips in English classes.
8. I have been working late lately.
9. I have been doing exercise every other day.
10. I have been doing a part time job as a clerk at a convenience store.

Unit 6

Pattern practice answers

I.
1. He told her that she might go.
2. She asked me to call her later.
3. He asked who I talked to.
4. He told me that I came to his office then.
5. He proposed to celebrate his promotion that night.
6. She exclaimed that it was a very beautiful sight.
7. The man said with regret that it was all his fault.
8. The student said with joy that he passed the exam.
9. She expressed her wish that she may pass the exam.
10. She said that she would not go out that night, for it was

raining.

II.

(1) Well, I asked him if he loved extreme sports.
(2) Then I asked him if he loved animals.
(3) The best was when I asked him if he was seeing anybody.

III.

1. Harry said that he was looking forward to the election.
2. Alicia said that she didn't care about elections and president.
3. Tony and Lisa said that they wanted to talk to Alicia about the importance of voting.
4. Hector said that he would not vote because he couldn't vote online.

Audio script

A: Christina! How was your day?
B: Pretty good. There was a career fair at the college.
A: Oh, really? What was it like?
B: There were many executives from different companies giving information.
A: Sounds pretty well-organized. Did you have a chance to talk to anyone?
B: Yeah, I spoke to the personnel manager of a big IT company.
A: So, what did you find out?
B: She told me about the job possibilities for new graduates. She said that they hire about 25 new employees a year.
A: That's encouraging. Did you get any other information?
B: I asked her if they had offices in other area. She said they have offices in Hong Kong, Sydney and Tokyo.
A: Really? What else did she ask you?
B: She asked me what I planned to do after graduation.
A: So what did you tell her?
B: I told her I wasn't sure but I was very interested in a job overseas.
A: Good. Oh, by the way, Jason called a little while ago.
B: Did he leave a message?
A: He said he would call back later.
B: O.K. Thank you dad!

Listening comprehension answers

1. F   2. F   3. F   4. T   5. T

Reading comprehension

She is putting her life on hold after her fiancé's murder.

이든과 나는 고등학생 연인이었다. 우리는 사랑에 빠졌고 대학 3학년 때 결혼하기로 계획했었다. 그러나 신은 나에게 새로운 꿈을 주었다. 그 일이 일어난 건 내가 22살이 되기 전이었다. 이든은 여름방학 동안 인턴으로 일했고 모두에게 음료수를 사다 주기 위해 사무실을 비웠다. 해고된 어떤 남자가 이든을 쐈다. 그는 이든이 어떤 사람인지 거의 알지 못했다. 난 성스런 간섭이 내 인생을 바꾸어 놓았고 다른 인생항로에 놓이게 했다고 생각했다. 이든이 죽은 후에 난 어떻게 내 생각을 조절해야 하는지를 배웠다. 난 심각한 우울증으로 고생했다. 사건이 일어난 지 5년이 지난 후 난 내가 강해져서 모든 것으로부터 자유로워지고 과거를 놓아줄 수 있기를 희망했다. 몇 년이 지난 후에도 내가 가족을 갖는다는 생각으로 즐거워할 수가 없었다. 어느 날 밤 난 이든에 관한 꿈을 꾸었다. 난 그를 지하철역에서 만났다. 그는 나를 기다리고 있었고 난 그 옆에 앉았다. 꿈에서 그는 천국에 있다고 말했고 내가 앞으로 나갈 수 있기를 원한다고 말했다. 난 일어나서 그를 뒤돌아 보았고 그는 나에게 가라고 손을 저었다. 그 다음 날 아침 난 남자친구인 데이비드에게 전화해서 뉴욕으로 이사하자고 말했다. 우리는 결혼했고 지금은 쌍둥이가 있다. 난 이 우주 어딘가에 이든이 아직도 존재한다고 믿고 있다. 땅에 묻혔다고 해서 사랑이 없어지지는 않는다고 믿는다. 또 한 가지 내가 배운 사실은 아직도 세상에는 행복이 존재한다는 메시지를 범죄 희생자들에게 전하는 것이 중요하다는 것이다. 행복이 당신에게 올 테고 그것을 받아들여야 한다.

Reading comprehension answers

1. F 2. F 3. T
4. T 5. T

Sentence building

1. My boss told me that I might go.
2. My boyfriend asked me to call him later.
3. My girlfriend overheard me talk to the phone and asked who I talked to.
4. My professor told me that I stopped by his/her office then.
5. The player proposed to celebrate his victory that night.
6. When I visited Grand Cannon a couple of years ago, I exclaimed that it was such a beautiful scenery.
7. My friend broke up with her boyfriend recently and she said with regret that it was all her fault.
8. The student said with joy that she/he passed the interview to be an announcer.
9. I expressed my wish that my sister may/might pass the college entrance exam.
   I expressed my wish that my sister passed the exam.
   I wished that my sister had passed the exam.
10. I said that I would not go out last Saturday night, for it was raining.

Unit 7

Pattern practice answers

I.
1. too much; enough   2. enough ; too many/too much
3. enough   4. too much; enough   5. too

II.
1. little   2. little   3. fewer   4. little   5. less

Audio script

A: What's that on your shirt?
B: It's some tomato sauce. It's my favorite but it's little difficult to eat. Every time I eat this, I usually get some on my clothes.
A: How can you eat so many of those?
B: Oh, I don't eat that many. I just eat once every other week.
A: Well, there's too much tomato sauce and not enough cheese. I like a lot of cheese. Also, there is so much salt on those things and a lot of fat. That's not good for you.
B: Actually, I bought the unsalted kind. And I read that they're good for your heart.

Listening comprehension answers

1. tomato sauce
2. once in every other week
3. healthy

Reading comprehension

소금, 또는 소금 결정체라고 알려진 것은 주로 소듐 클로라이드라는 물질로 된 무기질이다. 약간의 소금은 동물의 생명에 필수적이지만 너무 많은 소금은 동물과 식물에 해롭다. 소금은 가장 오래되고 가장 흔한 양념이며 염장법은 중요한 식품 저장법이다. 짠맛은 인간이 느낄 수 있는 기본적인 맛의 일종이다. 인간이 소금을 소비할 때는 여러 가지 형태로 나타난다. 바닷소금, 정제 소금, 요오드 첨가 소금이다. 소금은 수정같이 생긴 단단하고 하얀, 연한 분홍색이나 약간의 회색을 띠고 보통 바닷물이나 바위 침전물에서 얻어진다. 식용의 바위소금은 미네랄을 함유하기 때문에 약간 회색을 띤다.

Reading comprehension answers

1. T   2. T   3. T
4. T   5. F

Sentence building

1. I eat too much fast food like hamburger and not enough healthy food such as fruits and vegetables./fruit and vegetable.
2. I'm not hungry enough to eat dinner because I ate too many snacks.
3. I never had enough time to study, so I failed the exam.
4. During my college days, I studied too much so that I didn't sleep much or eat enough.
5. I don't like raw fish because they're too smelly/they smell too bad.
6. Korean Cuisine has little fat.
7. There is little food in my refrigerator.
8. I try to eat the food containing fewer calories to lose weight/for diet.
9. I try to eat few carbohydrates/little carbohydrate these days.
10. I have to eat less fat for diet/to lose weight. I have to cut down fat.

Unit 8

Pattern practice answers

1. not less than   2. as   3. as   4. not so much
5. more   6. than   7. no more than
8. not less than   9. than   10. as

Audio script

A: Hi, Eric, I'm calling from Detroit.
B: Merry Christmas! What do you think Detroit?
A: It's great except for the weather. It's freezing cold.
B: As far as I know, it's much colder than Seoul. So, you don't like the climate! How do you like the night life?
A: It is less than Seoul. Especially, public transportation is terrible. It is not easy to live without a car. The nightclubs, Karaoke, and everything else is too far away from my apartment. Detroit is no more than a big city.
B: Seoul has twice the population of Detroit.
A: That's right! Anyway, I miss Seoul. The more I stay, the more I miss my home.
B: Did you find some place interesting?
A: Yes, I found a church as old as my great grandfather.
B: Really? That's interesting.

Listening comprehension answers

1. calling   2. what do you think
3. except for   4. much colder than
5. how do you like   6. less than
7. public transportation   8. no more than
9. more   10. as old as

Reading comprehension

지난 십 년간 더 나은 영양 덕분에 늘어난 한국 어린이들의 키와 몸무게의 성장이 약간 더디어졌다. 교육과학기술부는 수요일에 2010학년도 전국의 747개교의 188,000명의 학생으로부터 조사한 건강설문지의 결과를 발표했다. 이에 따르면 한국의 어린이들은 20년 전의 한국 어린이들에 비해 6.4cm 더 크고, 10.54kg 더 무거운 것으로 나타났다. 그러나 어린이들의 키와 몸무게의 평균 성장은 눈에 띄게 느려졌다. 예를 들면, 1980년과 1990년 사이 6학년 남자아이의 평균 키는 4.79cm 성장했고 1990년과 2000년 사이에는 4cm, 2000년과 2010년 사이에는 단지 2.15cm 더 성장했다. 그리고 6학년 여자아이들의 몸무게도 1990년과 2000년 사이에는 4.79kg 늘었고 지난 10년 사이에는 2.65kg만 늘었다. 인제대학교 일산백병원의 유아청소년의학과 교수인 문진수 씨는 건강설문지 결과를 분석하여 어린이들이 자신의 부모보다 체격적으로 월등히 큰 세대 변화는 이제 거의 멈춘 것 같다고 말했다. 그는 한국인들의 유전적 특성과 현재의 환경(영양 및 기타환경)에 기인한 가능한 최대 성장이 이루어졌다고 말했다.

한국 어린이들의 평균 신장과 몸무게는 일본이나 중국 같은 다른 아시아 국가들의 어린이들에 비해 이미 크다고 문 교수는 덧붙였다. 그러나 아직도 수면 부족이나 운동 부족, 영양의 불균형 같은 문제들이 해결된다면 더 클 수 있는 가능성은 남아 있다고 했다.

Reading comprehension answers

1. T   2. F   3. T
4. T   5. F

Sentence building

1. She is as shy as foolish.
2. She is as happy as she can be after she married.
3. She swam as fast as she could in order to survive.
4. He is not so much a professor as a politician.
5. He has twice as much money as I have.
6. The longer I stay with him, the more I like him.
7. He is more clever than smart.
8. He is not richer than you are.
9. He has not more than 10 bucks.
10. He has not less than 100 bucks.

Unit 9

Pattern practice answers

I.

1. the largest   2. the fastest   3. the most tourism
4. the most famous   5. the best   6. the worst
7. the most flights

II.

1. long   2. wide   3. large   4. hot   5. deep

Audio script

A: Welcome to Travel Talk. I'm your host. My guest today is travel writer Ray Lopez. Ray has traveled around the world and his new book is called A Traveler's Treasure. Welcome to our show.

B: Thank you for having me today. It's great to be here.

A: Ray, Let's talk about your new book. Tell me, what's the most interesting place you've ever been to?

B: Well, one really interesting place I've visited is Machu Picchu, Peru. It's the most unusual ancient city. There's a picture of it in my book.

A: Now, you've been to some beautiful natural places, too. What's the most beautiful place you've seen?

B: Hmmm—. That's a difficult question. There are so many beautiful places. Well, Monterey Bay has the most beautiful natural features I've ever seen.

A: Yea, it sure does. O.K. Let's talk about your best and worst vacations. What's the best vacation you've had?

B: My trip to Bryce Canyon, Utah last year was the best vacation. It was absolutely amazing. Here's a picture of the canyon.

A: Wow! What was the most exciting thing you've done on a trip?

B: Mountain bike trail. It was the most exciting thing I've ever done.

A: I bet. Now I have to ask, what was your worst vacation?

B: Well, two years ago, I went to the Dead horse point. It was a beautiful canyon and I was supposed to go hiking with my friends. But I was very sick with the flu. I had to stay in a hotel room for three days. I didn't see or do anything. It was the worst trip.

A: Yeah, it sure sounds terrible. Ray. I want to thank you for being on our show.

B: You're welcome. It was my pleasure.

Listening comprehension answers

1. the most unusual ancient city.
2. the most beautiful natural features
3. It was absolutely amazing.
4. Mountain bike trail. It was the most exciting thing I've ever done.

5. very sick with the flu. I had to stay in a hotel room for three days.

Reading comprehension

아직 열악한 상태의 보전과 대부분이 발굴되지 않은 상태이지만 코바 고고학공원은 방대한 체계의 의식을 위한 길과 외부와 단절된 정글 풍경과 유카탄 반도에서 제일 큰 피라미드를 포함한 여러 개의 흥미로운 피라미드들로 주목할 만하다. 멕시코의 유카탄 반도의 거친 동부의 반쪽에 위치한 코바 지역은 툴럼이라 도시에서 버스나 차로 한 시간 정도 거리에 있다.

Reading comprehension answers

1. F 2. T 3. T

Sentence building

1. What is the worst problem for university students these days?
2. Which city has the largest population?
3. The more stress you get, the worse your grade you have.
4. How long is the Mississippi River?
5. What is the least expensive gift?
6. How tall is your cousin?
7. The Brice Cannon is the most famous for its beauty and about 20 kilometers wide.
8. The Nile River is 6,695 kilometers long.
9. Which school has the largest number of students in Korea?
10. How hot does it get in Sahara Desert?

Unit 10

Pattern practice answers

1. don't you   2. doesn't he   3. isn't he
4. aren't you   5. hasn't it   6. shall we?
7. will you   8. won't you   9. hadn't you
10. didn't they

Audio script

Background information

Old friends are gathering at a school reunion party.

A: It feels so strange to be back here, doesn't it?
B: Sure it is. I guess everything has changed.
A: But not this bench. It looks the same, doesn't it?
B: Yeah! Exactly! Do you remember when we used to come here at lunch time?
A: Of course. We used to come here almost every day.
B: When was the day we had a fight?
A: It was the last Friday of November, wasn't it?
B: Why did we fight?
A: It was about Pamela, wasn't it?
B: Really? Why?
A: She was so popular at that time. She looks so different now, doesn't she?
B: Yeah! I remember now. She broke your heart.
A: I should have accepted your advice at that time.
B: I am glad that you see the truth now.

Listening comprehension answers

1. bench   2. lunchtime   3. a girl

Reading comprehension

사회적 계층 이동은 고혈압을 방지할 수 있다고 한 연구 결과가 제시됐다. 스웨덴의 연구자들은 12,000명의 동성 쌍둥이들의 혈압과 그들과 부모의 사회적 지위를 조사해서 '전염병학과 지역사회 건강'이라는 학회지에 기고했다. 낮은 사회, 경제적 지위에서 태어나 나중에 더 나은 사회 계층으로 이동한 쌍생아들은 그대로 가난한 사회 계층에 남아 있는 쌍생아들보다 고혈압이 생긴 사례가 훨씬 적게 나타났다.

영국의 전문가들은 건강에 있어 사회 계층간의 차이를 줄이기 위한 조치가 필요하다고 말했다. 고혈압은 심장 질환과

뇌출혈을 일으키는 요인으로 알려져 있다. 그러나 더 높은 사회, 경제적 그룹으로 이동하는 것의 효과는 알려져 있지 않다. 한 이론은 자신의 가족과 함께 자란 사람들과 다른 사회 계층으로 이동하는 것은 더 많은 스트레스를 유발한다고 하고, 어떤 이론가들은 더 나은 사회계층으로 이동하는 것 자체가 건강을 지킬 수 있는 기회를 늘린다고 주장한다.

이 연구에서 Karolinska연구소의 연구자들은 1926년에서 1958년 사이에 태어난 12,000명의 동성 쌍생아들의 부모와 그들이 성인이 된 후의 사회, 경제적 지위를 추적하기 위해 스웨덴의 쌍둥이 등록부에서 자료를 이용했다.

1973년도에 건강과 lifestyle에 대한 사후 조사가 이루어졌다. 생애 주기에 관한 조사의 일부로 전화 면담이 1998년과 2002년 사이에 이루어졌다. 질문은 고혈압 치료가 있었는지를 포함했다. 부모의 직업은 스웨덴에서는 통상적으로 이러한 자료를 포함하는 출생증명서로부터 얻어졌다.

Reading comprehension answers

1. T   2. T   3. T

Sentence building

1. You live in Paris, don't you?
2. She works at a bank, isn't she?
3. He is moving near Seoul, isn't he?
4. You're practicing yoga recently, aren't you?
5. It has been three months, hasn't it?
6. Let's toast, shall we?
7. Come to my office now, will you?
8. Have a seat, won't you?
9. You'd better go home, hadn't you?
10. They used to go to school, didn't they?

Unit 11

Pattern practice answers

1. to go   2. to sleep   3. smoking
4. saying   5. to help   6. traveling
7. of telling   8. smoking   9. going
10. of giving

Audio script

A: My girlfriend always wants me to pay the meal when we have date; but I cannot afford to buy a meal every time.
B: Why don't you tell her frankly?
A: I can't because I pretended to be rich.
B: Oh, No! She will find out that you are not rich eventually. Honesty is the best policy in a relationship.
A: I know; but I don't want to lose her. I really like her. If I tell her the truth, she will avoid seeing me.
B: If you lose her because you are not rich, she doesn't deserve you. You can't keep her with lying.
A: That's right. I will tell her the truth.

Listening comprehension answers

1. He cannot afford to pay the expenses when they are dating.
2. being honest with her.

Reading comprehension

집을 사시나요? 사소한 실수가 과소비, 구두협약 등 여러분의 기막힌 협상을 망칠 수 있다. 매도인이 들을 수 있는 거리에서 재산(살 집)에 대해 개인적인 말을 하는 것은 비록 매수인이 집을 살 수 있는 경제적 능력이 있다 하더라도 장래의 매수인을 좌절시킬 수 있다. 이것은 주택을 사는 사람들에 의해 이루어지는 가장 흔한 실수라고 언급하는 국제 부동산 그룹의 사장인 마이크 베스터 씨의 충고다.

사람들의 새집을 향상시키거나 개인화하고자 하는 열망을 이해하지만 마이크 베스터 씨는 집을 사고자 하는 사람들은 매도인이 있는 자리에서 벽을 허문다든가, 나무를 없앤다든가, 거실을 아이들 게임룸으로 바꾼다든가 하는 등에 관한 말을 삼가야 한다고 주의를 준다. 베스터 씨는 매도인은 자신들의 집에 대해 매우 감상적이어서 매수인이 필요한 존중을 보여주지 않으면 고집스러워져서 협상하기 힘들 수도 있다고 말한다.

이것은 매도인을 기분 상하게 하는 위험을 감소시킬 뿐만 아니라 남아 있는 감정이 판단을 흐리게 하고 무리한 기대감을 만들 수도 있기 때문에 집중하기 위해서도 필요하다고 덧붙였다. 매수인들은 가끔 티 하나 없이 완벽한 집을 소유하고 싶어서 부동적이 됩니다. 그러나 현실적으로 매수인들은 매도인을 화나게 하는 것을 피하고 싶다면 집을 관리해야 하고 그러기 위해 수리나 변경이 언제든지 필요하다는 것을 받아들여야 합니다.

Reading comprehension answers
1. F 2. F 3. T
4. T 5. F

Sentence building
1. I cannot afford to buy expensive gifts for my girlfriend.
2. My grandfather pretended to sleep when I visited him.
3. He gave up finding his job because of his health.
4. I tried to avoid making too many promises.
5. I was trying to help her; but I ended up screwing her life.
6. I prefer traveling by airplane rather than ship.
7. I am afraid of telling her the truth because I might lose her.
8. I stopped exercising because the doctor told me to.
9. I regret not going to the Philippines last winter.
10. I choose not to live in America.

Unit 12

Pattern practice answers
I.
1. with 2. of 3. at
4. in 5. from

II.
1. X 2. X 3. O
4. X 5. O

Audio script
A: Hey, Martha. Do you want to go to a concert with me next week?
B: Well, maybe. Who's playing?
A: It's a famous band. Have you heard of this song? (tuning)
B: Who composed it?
A: It was composed by Berv Mac Kathy. The leader of this group.
B: O.K. I guess I know this song. But I didn't know this song was composed by this band.
A: I just got free tickets. You know Amy. She is going with us. We're going to go after work.
B: Doesn't she have a boyfriend? Martin!
A: Oh, she was dumped by him recently. You'd better not to mention about it when we go out with Amy.
B: O.K. Thanks for the tip.

Listening comprehension answers
1. They are going to a concert.
2. Amy and Martin broke up recently.

Reading comprehension
태국의 의회는 새로운 수상, Abhisit Vejjajiva를 선출함으로써 논란의 여지가 많은 전 수상과 깊숙이 관련된 연합정부를 끝냈다. 시위자들은 선거가 끝난 후 의회 건물 밖에서 국가의 깊은 정치적 양분이 남아 있다는 사인을 들고 시위했다. 태국의 반대파 지도자인 Abhisit Vejjajiva는 2008년 9월 12일 방콕의 의회수상을 선거하기 위해 참석했다. 연합정부의 지도자인 44세의 Abhisit 씨는 태국의 27번째 수상이 될 것이다. 그의 이번 선거는 전 수상인 Thaksin Shinawatra 씨와 관련된 연합된 정부의 1년간 통치를 끝내게 될 것이다. 많은 태국인들은 월요일의 선거가 몇 달간 지속된 정치적 긴장을 끝내기를 희망한다. 이러한 긴장은 이달 초 수천 명의 반정부시위자들이 수상의 집무실 건물을 장악하기 위해 드러눕고 방콕 공항을 봉쇄했을 때 악화되었다.

Chulalongkorn대학의 경제학교수인 Sompob Manarangsan 씨는 이번 선거가 태국의 민주화에 대한 자신감을 회복하는 데 도움을 줄 것이라고 말한다.

Reading comprehension answers

1. F 2. T 3. T

Sentence building

1. The Cow was painted with oil painting.
2. He was taken good care of by his wife.
3. The boy was upset because he was laughed at by his classmates.
4. Flowers were brought for her by her boyfriend as a birthday present.
   Flowers were brought by her boyfriend as a birthday present for her.
5. The nuclear bomb was used in 1945.
6. The Thinker was sculpted from bronze.
7. The ball was thrown for his son by him.
   The ball was thrown by him for his son.
8. She was denied entrance to the U.S. by the immigration officer.
9. The most expensive furniture in my house was sold by me for my neighbor.
10. He is becoming a monster as time goes by.

Unit 13

Pattern practice answers

1. cannot be   2. must be   3. used to
4. am used to   5. had better   6. should
7. of   8. obey   9. take   10. stupid

Audio script

A: What's the problem? You don't look good!
B: I have a terrible headache every night. I can't sleep.
A: When was the last time you went to the doctor?
B: I can't remember.
A: You'd better see a doctor right now.
B: But I am so sorry that I should take a day off. It is difficult of me to have day off. I am extremely busy at work these days.
A: How long have you had this problem?
B: It started last Monday. It has been almost a week. It's very painful. I've done everything I can. I took Tylenol and hot bath, but nothing seems to work.
A: So a headache and this causes the sleeping problem. You must be stressed out. It is wise that you should take a day off and relax. I suggest you that you should leave the work temporarily and travel somewhere. It will refresh your mind and body. It is stupid of you to keep working in this condition. If I were you, I would get plenty of rest.
B: O.K. I understand. I will follow your advice. Thank you buddy!

Listening comprehension answers

1. He can't sleep because of a headache.
2. He is extremely busy at work.
3. stress
4. a week
5. take day off and travel

Reading comprehension

한국 인구는 다른 나라에 비해 고령화가 빨리 진행되고 있다. 그러나 이러한 걱정스러운 추세에 대한 영향을 다루는 데 가장 준비가 안 된 나라일 것이다. 미국의 외교정책고문인 '전략과 국제학 연구소'의 연구에 의하면 한국은 수입적 합지수에 관해 설문 조사한 20개 국가 중 19위를 기록했다고 일요일에 '전략재정부'가 발표했다. 설문조사는 수입적합지수와 재정 안정성이라는 2개의 지표를 사용했다. 이 지표는 각 나라가 얼마나 잘 노령 인구를 다룰 준비가 되어 있는지를 재는 데 중요하다. 한국은 중국보다 하나 뒤처지고 멕시코보다 앞선 채로 거의 꼴등을 기록했다. 재정 안정성 지표만 12위를 기록해서 조금 낫다. 이 지표는 국가가 점점 늘고 있는 노령 인구를 먹여 살릴 수 있는 재정적 여유가 있는지를 고려하는 지표라고 '전략과 국제학 연구소'가 말했다. 한국은 이제 이 두 가지 범주에서 낮게 기록한 프랑스와 이태리와 비슷한 처지이다. 이러한 국가들은 자신들을 먹여 살리기 위해 충분한 돈을 벌 수 없는 그러나 각각의 재정적 제한으로 현재 근근이 지탱하고 있는 노인들을 도와주기 위해 국가 재정을 투입해야 하는 필요성으로 고군분투하고 있다.

'전략과 국제학 연구소'는 한국은 연금자금저축을 격려하고 노인들을 재정적 위험에서 구제하기 위해 사회보장제도를 강화하고 출산율을 증가시키고 이민을 장려해야 한다고 조언했다.

Reading comprehension answers

1. T 2. F 3. F
4. T 5. T

Sentence building

1. Jane cannot be her younger sister. Jane looks much older than her sister.
2. She must be her mother. Christina resembles her mother.
3. It is very polite of you to say so.
4. The teacher insisted that every student should follow his method.
5. I used to skip the breakfast in the morning.
6. He was used to being laughed at.
7. I'd better do the homework now rather than do it later.
8. It is necessary that he should apply for a job as much as possible.
9. It is stupid that he believes her story.
   It is stupid of him to believe her story.
10. It is convenient of him to change the rule.

Unit 14

Pattern practice answers

1. reading   2. wearing   3. excited
4. exciting   5. touched   6. barking
7. tailed   8. disappointed 9. crying
10. colored

Audio script

A: Do you have any plans for this weekend?
B: I don't think anything special comes up. How about you? What are you planning to do?
A: I'm going to go to a bookstore. One of my favorite authors will have the signing ceremony for the audience.
B: Oh, really? That sounds exciting. You must be excited.
A: Yes, I am so thrilled about it. Would you like to go with me?
B: Oh, sure. When is it?
A: Saturday at two O'clock.
B: That's too bad. I have a previous engagement.
A: Oh, I'm so disappointed. You said you didn't have anything special. Can you cancel the appointment?
B: No, way! I almost forgot. I have planned it for three months. I'm so sorry to make you disappointed.
A: Well, that's O.K.
B: But thanks for asking. Let's do something another time, O.K.?

Listening comprehension answers

1. Go to a bookstore.
2. One of his favorite authors will have the signing ceremony for the audience.

3. She has a previous engagement.
4. To cancel the appointment.

9. I saw her wearing a red dress at the party.
10. I watched the exciting TV program last weekend.

Reading comprehension

점점 더 많은 수의 북한군 장교와 군인들이 막사에서 한국 영화나 드라마를 보다가 적발되고 있다고 소식통이 전했다. 북한을 자주 방문하는 베이징에 기반을 둔 한 소식통은 월요일에 다음과 같이 말했다. 여러 명의 육군 장교와 사병들이 작년부터 남한 영화나 TV 드라마를 보다가 적발되었고 군에서는 모든 장교와 사병들에게 제국주의의 문화적 침투를 방지하기 위한 집중적인 교화 프로그램을 제공하고 있다.

북한의 군사 기강과 도덕성이 국제적인 제재하에 서서히 파괴되고 있고, 한 장교는 북한과 중국 국경지역에서 DVD를 팔다가 적발되었다.

군 기강의 약화는 주로 2009년 후반에 실패한 화폐개혁 이후의 경제적 어려움에 기인한다. 음식물의 부족은 민간에서 음식을 수집할 수 없게 됨에 따라 막사에서 더욱 심해지고 있다.

베이징에 기반을 둔 중국 북한 전문가는 북한군의 자원을 분배하는 능력이 작년 전당대회 이후 정권이 그 우선권을 군대에서 당으로 이양했기 때문이라고 말했다.

Reading comprehension answers

1. T   2. T   3. T
4. F   5. T

Sentence building

1. The man reading a book is the principal of this school.
2. The wounded patient is taken care of by a nurse at a hospital.
3. I saw her crossing the street in the intersection.
4. I thought the game would be exciting, but I was bored.
5. Don't wake up a sleeping baby.
6. Tax should be reduced for the retired employees.
7. I will fix the broken window by noon.
8. Frankly speaking, he is not a wise man.

Acknowledgement

언제나 제 옆에서 지지해주는 사랑하는 남편 Eric, 바쁜 엄마에게 불평도 없이 자기 할 일 잘하는 착한 우리 아이들 Eddie와 Mirae, 저를 위해 항상 기도해 주시는 어머니와 가족들, 멀리 떨어져 있어도 기도로 힘을 주시는 우리 시아버님, 시어머님 Michael& Denise Palmateer, 믿음 단추 버튼을 누르고 잘 따라와 주는 성결대학교 영문과 학생들, 동료 교수님들, 책 출간을 도와주신 출판사 여러분, 이 책이 나오기까지 많은 도움을 주신 여러분들께 감사를 드립니다.

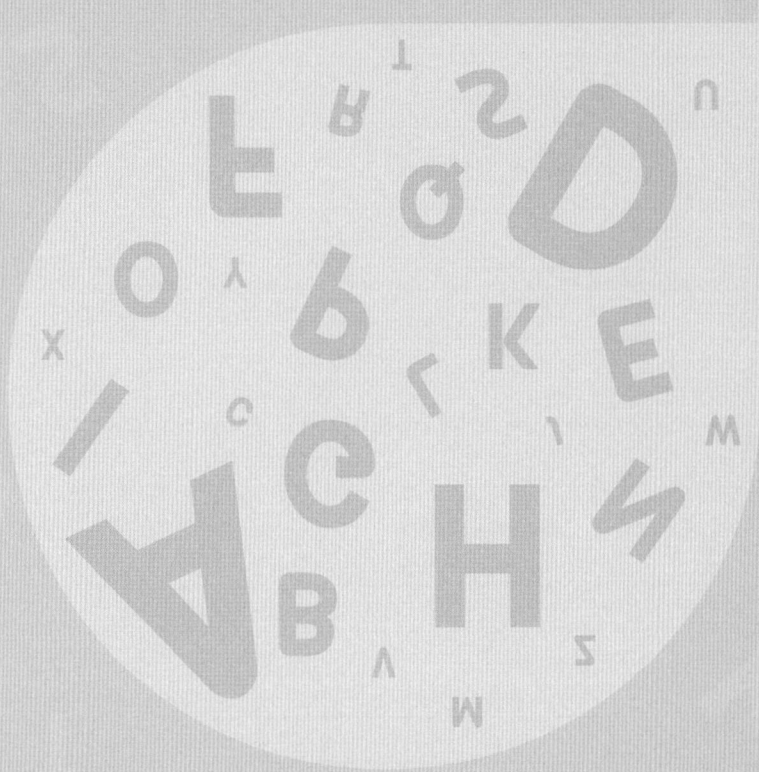

회화를 위한 거꾸로 영문법

초판 1쇄 발행일 2013년 2월 6일

지은이 이정아
펴낸이 박영희
편집 이은혜·유태선·정지선·김미령
인쇄·제본 에이피프린팅
펴낸곳 도서출판 어문학사
　　　서울특별시 도봉구 쌍문동 523-21 나너울 카운티 1층
　　　대표전화: 02-998-0094 / 편집부1: 02-998-2267, 편집부2: 02-998-2269
　　　홈페이지: www.amhbook.com
　　　트위터: @with_amhbook
　　　블로그: 네이버 http://blog.naver.com/amhbook
　　　　　　 다음 http://blog.daum.net/amhbook
　　　e-mail: am@amhbook.com
　　　등록: 2004년 4월 6일 제7-276호

ISBN 978-89-6184-289-1 18740
정가 12,000원

이 도서의 국립중앙도서관 출판시도서목록(CIP)은 e-CIP홈페이지(http://www.nl.go.kr/ecip)와
국가자료공동목록시스템(http://www.nl.go.kr/kolisnet)에서 이용하실 수 있습니다.
(CIP제어번호: CIP2013000109)

※잘못 만들어진 책은 교환해 드립니다.